How to Make Mistakes

The One-Minute Guide to Winning at Losing

Roger J. Brown

Copyright © 2021 Roger J. Brown

All rights reserved.

ISBN:978-0-9850755-6-9

DEDICATION

This book is dedicated to the memory of all the rednecks whose last words were:

"Hey, y'all, watch THIS!"

How to Make Mistakes

CONTENTS

	Foreword	i
1	Kinds of Mistakes	1
2	Mistakes with Relatives	9
3	Mistakes with Partners	15
4	Mistakes with Money	27
5	Mistakes with Computers	33
6	Mistakes with Government	39
7	Mistakes with Real Estate	49
8	Mistakes with Education	55
9	Mistakes with Health	61
10	Mistakes with Climate	67
11.	Mistakes with Aging	75
12.	Mistakes with Religion	81
13.	A Case Study in Mistakes	87
	Afterword	115

FOREWORD

What is a Foreword? Why is it written last and appears first? What does it have to do with "Forward"? Heady questions, all, but not ones answered in this book.

Typically, the Foreword is written by someone other than the author. I thought of asking a friend to write one for me, if I had any friends. My guess is that someone would write something like "I tried to keep him from being an insufferable moralist but failed so this is what you get." I then realized I could write that myself.

Maybe a Foreword is there to try to get people to read the Introduction. Isn't that redundant?

Sometimes a Foreword answers the question: Why write this book? No luck here. It is not at all clear the world needs something that sounds like Friedrich Nietzsche met Will Cuppy or a TED talk by Aunt Blabby, but here you have it. There is a wonderful book I read recently by Jordan Ellenberg titled <u>How Not To Be Wrong: The Power of Mathematical Thinking</u>. Mine is sort of the complement to Jordan's book. Hold ON!! I said, what about all those people who *want to be wrong*? It is a crime to neglect that significant population. If you are one of these people you have landed right where you should be.

So, the Foreword warns the reader. It shares some of the better qualities of the overall book itself: Short. It also gives clues about what you can find if you read further. For instance, sprinkled throughout the footnotes is a reading list of books the author has found helpful in recognizing many of his own mistakes, after the fact, of course.

In this little book I demonstrate what one can do during retirement to try to leave behind some hints to those who follow. My life has been the combination of hard work, luck, hard work, maybe a smattering of intelligence, hard work and hard work. Did I mention "hard work"? No matter what you conclude from reading this book, know that you can overcome all your mistakes by hard work. I know it is out of style to recommend something so simple and prosaic in these days of trending and branding and chilling. But if you are just an average nincompoop like me, it is a real life saver. My grandfather told me that work will never hurt you.

He was right.

So, take a chance. Turn the page. What's the worst that can happen? You, too, can overcome your stumbles and missteps as I have. What follows is a compendium of minor rants by one of our nation's most justifiably unsung heroes. Here is just one thought to inspire you: I have given up self-deprecating humor.

Because I am no good at it.

RJB

San Diego, CA
Winter, 2021

1 - KINDS OF MISTAKES

Warning – Graphic Content: This book contains political incorrectness. It also contains some mathematics. If you are sensitive to either of these, please return this book to wherever you got it. I do not want to hurt anyone's feelings. There are "trigger words" sprinkled liberally throughout. Some material may be unsuitable for sensitive persons. I can't figure out who these people are, so my best recommendation for anyone with a squeamish nature is to find an old copy of the Saturday Evening Post to read instead of this book.

We need a Handbook of Mistakes to help people who have forgotten how. There is an alarming shortage of mistakes because we now live in a world where nothing is wrong. Mistakes are an endangered species in need of saving. We need a bumper sticker that says, "Save the Mistakes!"

There is also BIG MONEY in mistakes. People have found a new way to riches through screwing up. Make a mess of your life and you can get other people to support you. Or at least you can get politicians *to promise* to take other people's money and give it to you. You do not even have to wait for some TV reporter to put a microphone in your face and ask you "How did you feel when you realized you *[insert actual bonehead event here]* ?" Get a friend with a cellphone camera, record your idiocy and put it up on YouTube. Think of it. Fame, fortune, followers, everything a world class loser can ask for. It can all be yours.

The place to begin, I suppose, is putting mistakes in their proper place by listing the sorts of mistakes that need to be made. But before I do that I need to point out a mistake I only discovered when writing this book. A common mistake is not recognizing you have made a mistake.  Prior to publication this tome was previewed by a focus group made up of some of the finest illiterate homeless people to be found anywhere. Four out of five of these luminaries failed to see the mistake on the front cover. If you are looking back at the cover about now, congratulations. You are in the majority!

So, back to a mistake taxonomy…

In broad categories there are errors of *omission* – something you forget, overlook or leave out – and errors of *commission* – things you actually do that are wrong. There is also the confusing but important distinction between the wrong thing to do and doing something wrong. The former has to do with choosing among alternatives and picking the wrong one; the latter has to do with the poor execution of whatever choice you make. It is a mistake to think these are the same thing. Doing them together is glorious. Not many people can choose the wrong thing and then do that badly. Your friends and family will be in awe should you accomplish this. You could even aspire to the Mistake Triathlon where you do the wrong thing badly at the wrong time. Only the truly gifted can accomplish this feat, almost never twice.

Fear not, even if you are not a connoisseur of such fine points you will have no difficulty screwing up in all categories if you read this book AND if you live long enough.

There are mistakes that are harmless. They hurt no one. The cover of the book is an example. There are mistakes that are not harmless to others, hurting only you. My writing this book would be an example if it were possible for my reputation to fall any lower.

We should all avoid mistakes that are harmful to

others, especially those harmful to everyone. With the help of this book you may be able to avoid that.

Another way to classify mistakes is how easily are they rectified. Mistakes can be easy or hard to fix. They can be costly to fix. Some may be impossible to fix. It is best to avoid those mistakes lest you pay for the rest of your life.

A special category needs to be carved out for mistakes that are *only* costly to fix. When nothing but money – your money – is involved, the lesson a costly mistake provides can be priceless. Add lawyers to the mix and the cost multiplies (the true purpose of lawyers is to increase the cost of things) leaving a trail of monetary tears that is impossible to forget.

Mistakes can be local or global. Obviously, system-wide mistakes are bad. It takes a real genius to foul up something that reaches far from where the dunderhead sits.

Some mistakes are technical in nature. We can consider these in the most practical sense. It is a mistake to add 2 + 2 and get 5. Then there are theoretical mistakes, things fundamentally wrong in principle. It is a different mistake to *continue to believe* that 2+2 = 5 even after someone who knows the truth explains otherwise. Too many repeats of this one suggests that *you* may be a mistake. Many people have highly developed abilities to ignore physical realities while screwing up. Some of these people used to take selfies while leaning backward over a cliff.

Thus far we have merely considered the individual idiot wandering around bumping into things. But whole societies of such people can institutionalize mistakes, spreading the misery farther and faster than any one Dufus could ever hope. For instance, the construction of a political economy amounts to agreeing on a system of rules to conduct civil order. It is only slight over-simplification to say that the aggregate effort of dumb voters leads to chaos and breakdown of society. But they can't do it alone. The mob also needs misguided potentates, demagogues and other manipulators (see: Congressional Action) to raise stupidity to that order of magnitude. Look around and you won't have to look far to see that an ignorant electorate and a cabal of dumb politicians represent a potent route to calamity.

Staying with the idea of Groupdumb (a natural consequence of Groupthink) for a moment, it is worth noting that many forms of policing are less effective than a good set of incentives and remedies. So, for instance, most people think the Highway Patrol enforces traffic laws. Not true. Insurance companies enforce traffic laws. Actually, even insurance companies are secondary. Self-preservation comes first. Until cellphones were invented people stopped at red lights not because they thought they would get a ticket or their insurance premium would increase, but because they did not want to be killed in an accident. Young people who read their email while driving think they are immortal. Tragically, some of them learn, *in situ*, that this is a mistake.

Here we must digress into mistakes that are fatal. Everyone tries to avoid these. Perhaps the best reason to be extra careful to avoid these mistakes is that they can end your opportunity to make more mistakes. Think about your family before you do anything that stupid. They have enjoyed years of watching you screw up and are looking forward to many more years in which you provide them with endless entertainment. Is it fair to them to have to go back to watching Duck Dynasty for their periodic dose of stupidity?

Another way to characterize mistakes is to think about the number of situations that can lead to mistakes. In chapters that follow you will learn how to maximize mistakes made with relatives, spouses, teachers, government and money. Some of these mistakes are real dandies you won't want to miss. Some are practically unavoidable so you CANNOT miss making them. Various institutions have wired the system for their own benefit in ways designed to ensnare you in mistakes. Depending on how old you are you already know some of these traps that have been carefully set for you by the stupidity or perfidy of others.

Here is a perfect example of a mistake your author made that really happened. When I was very young,

I had the good fortune to receive a small scholarship to college from a service organization located near my high school. For the moment we won't dwell on what a mistake that was. Three or four years later as I was nearing the end of my undergraduate work in a college about 100 miles away from my high school, I received a letter from my sponsor. They were having a meeting and wanted to invite me to join them and tell them of my experience in higher education, a sort of reality check on how well their money was being spent. They sent me an invitation in the form of a letter (back in those days snail mail was all we had) from the organization's program chairman. So, I get a piece of mail from Barney Goodfellow, the opening line of which read "I have been appointed the Program Chairman of the [name of hapless service organization] and would like to invite you to…" What, you ask, could possibly go wrong with that? Never mind my having gotten excellent grades in English, in haste I misread the first line as '*You* have been appointed the Program Chairman…" My immediate thought was how odd since I was not a member of their secret society, did not live nearby and probably was not the best choice for this position. Nonetheless, I picked up the phone and called the author of the letter. The conversation that ensued probably did nothing to convince them they had made a good choice to receive the benefit of their largess and may have led to them terminating the scholarship program entirely. My thanking him for the honor of the appointment but having to decline due to distance and time constraints all got out before the depth and breadth of my error revealed itself.

That was an example of a comparatively harmless and perhaps humorous mistake that shattered no lives but tends to stay with you. It is for that reason that to this day I read e-mails twice before sending. You will be shocked to learn that I even read this Turkey twice.

In summary, making mistakes offers a rich menu of choices shared by virtually all of society. The incautious mixing of the stew of ignorance results in what you observe around you each day. Avoiding the potholes in life is a reasonable goal for which I wish you the best of luck.

Even as you read this someone is carving out a pothole beneath you. Let's meet some of these people now.

2 - MISTAKES WITH RELATIVES

The best place to start is close to home. Where do mistakes begin? Of course, you learn them from your parents. More generally, you learn them from your family. Relatives are a BIG source of mistake training. Some mistakes are handed down from generation to generation. Culture exists to perpetuate mistakes. Look at the DNA of any line and it will contain evidence of mistakes going back eons. Use 21st Century DNA tracking technology and you can find mistakes your parents forgot to mention. This can lead to meeting new people which can then introduce you to branches of your family, previously unknown, who are stretching the *panneaux* of dense behavior farther than you ever imagined. DNA is Nature's way of making sure mistakes remain healthy, vibrant and are passed along throughout all of time.

Most people dread the phrase "You become your parents" because they really don't want to do that. Around sixteen years of age people go through a period of rebellion, trying to avoid becoming their parents. About ten years later, married with children of their own, all of this is gone, and the well-worn track is being worn smoother and deeper than the prior generation did. So how does this jive with the overarching premise of this book, which is that mistakes are a dying breed? Simple. Parents, try though they may to teach their children not to make the mistakes they did, realize it is hopeless and find creative ways to ignore, forgive, or explain away their children's mistakes as "normal" or "growing pains" or "acting out." This is a really big mistake that spawns further mistakes. Not requiring children to take responsibility for their mistakes masks them and re-labels them as something they are not. It is a mistake to try to preserve children's' self-esteem by covering for their mistakes. Your child is not a genius. He or she is just an ordinary schmuck trying to avoid being run down by a train. Forgive yourself. You probably did the best you could.

In some cases, the parents are not the primary source of mistake training. Siblings, cousins, aunts and uncles all participate. Proximity determines how much these ancillary relatives contribute. Think about who you are closest to. Is it a parent or a brother or an aunt? That person may be your natural role model. With almost no effort you could be that person.

It is probably a good idea to rank your relatives to help you identify the biggest nitwit. Take a close look at their living circumstances. Living in their car is a clue. But it does not have to be so obvious. You probably have relatives with big houses and big garages with a lot of cars in them. They can be just as good a source of mistakes as anyone. If your relatives have a lot of *things* and are not happy, this is a mistake. It may look on the surface like a mistake you would like to make but it really isn't. It is true that money doesn't buy happiness. Nor does it buy smart, as Felicity Huffman will tell you.

Sometimes the best qualified, most mistake-free soul in your family is the quietest. He is the one you hear from the least. He is just getting up every morning (probably early) and going out into the world, doing what must be done and coming home (probably late) very tired. He looks like a plodder, sort of uninspiring, certainly not flashy, just a regular guy. He probably made some mistakes but took pains to make sure each time was a *different* mistake. Follow him around for a while and learn from him. You can learn some interesting mistakes and, with practice, you can be like him.

Most people have both male and female relatives. It would be a mistake to have only one or the other (it would also make the news). Without taking thunder from the forthcoming chapter devoted entirely to making mistakes with members of the opposite sex, it would be wise, when ranking world-class mistake makers in the family, to keep the two separate.

Mistakes made by women often involve men and vice-versa. The primary difference is that mistakes made by men tend to be louder and are remembered longer by women. Men take several decades more than women to escape their teen years, so there is this rich field of blunderism much larger and longer for men.

We have a saying in our family that nothing is so bad that Uncle Roger can't make it worse. To support this sentiment, I once cautioned a very bright nephew of mine against giving money to higher education, especially if he had to borrow to do it. I told him that colleges were full of some of the least inspiring dweebs God had ever invented, many of whom had jobs only because they had learned how to milk a political game to its fullest.

We have Mental Institutions, Penal Institutions and Academic Institutions, all places to put people who just do not fit into society anywhere else. For all these reasons I did not want my nephew making the mistake of encouraging academic slackers by giving them money. This resulted in his temporary impoverishment as a student. But I have faith in him. He is young and still has time to make lots of mistakes, even if I am not there to help.

How to Make Mistakes

3 - MISTAKES WITH PARTNERS

Let's go ahead and get it out of the way. This chapter involves sort of a sub-class of the prior chapter. After all, spouses and partners are relatives. But they constitute a special case for two reasons:

1. You pick them, unlike your relatives who are handed to you without your consent; and
2. You (at least for a time) ascribe to them certain magical qualities.

There are so many chances to make mistakes in this area it boggles the mind.

Selection

The math of the biology is worth mentioning here. Nature wants a diverse gene pool. So, the popular phrase "opposites attract" is code for: Mistake in progress. There are about 7 billion people on the planet of all shapes, colors, temperament, education, age… Well, you get the idea. Finding the right person who fits your shape, color, temperament, etc. for more than five minutes is an heroic task. Count the different ways 7 billion people may be paired. It is a very large number. What is the probability you will do this, especially at a young age, in a way that does not lead to disaster? The answer is a very small number. Contemplate these two numbers for a moment and you understand why the whole Rating-Dating-Mating game is huge crap shoot. Coupling incorrectly should not even qualify as a mistake since it is so common. Accounting has "contra assets" for this sort of thing. Maybe screwing up a relationship should be given the special category of "contra mistake." That way when you accidentally get it right all your divorced and bitter friends don't think you have just made a lucky mistake.

The best way to approach pairing up is to EXPECT to make a mistake. It is so easy to do and so often done it really takes no talent at all. If your goal is to make a world-class mistake this activity is RIPE for you. Just crank up those hormones to warp speed, stand back and watch your life get warped.

Ownership

W.C. Fields is credited with saying "Women are like elephants, I like to look at 'em but I wouldn't want to own one."[1] Perhaps the Grand Daddy of all romantic mistakes is to latch onto someone and conclude that you have made an acquisition. Owning another person is a mistake. Thinking you can own another person is just as big a mistake. From the instant you begin exercising your rights as an owner, at that second your partner will begin squirming to find a way to escape your grip. Or, worse, once you exercise your ownership rights you find you have a dependent. This is why my advice to my male friends looking for companionship has

---

[1] It is a mistake to attribute some pithy saying to the wrong person. Many people get credit or blame for saying things they never said. As far as I can tell W. C. Fields is the actual source for this. But it could be a mistake.

always been: Find a happy woman and LEAVE HER ALONE.

The fact that men and women are different introduces a whole host of new mistake opportunities beginning with the mistake of thinking men and women are different. Some people want to be different from the opposite sex, some people want to be the opposite sex, some people are just disgusted with the entire matter and would rather not think about it. Figuring out what category your target partner belongs in is a minefield. Your author is in the first category and knows he can't do anything about it. Advice from these pages is therefore tainted by a male perspective. As part of the Global admonishment that it is probably a mistake to believe anything you read here, I can't be much help. In addition to making choices about your own life, you are going to have to figure out which side the other party is on AND which side the other party *wants to be on* AND how long they will stay put on that side. Essentially, this has to be done simultaneously and instantaneously at first encounter. It can then either be seconds or years until one of you says "Mistakes were made…"

It really gets good when money is involved (see entire chapter below on making mistakes with money). Unlike people, money CAN be owned. In fact, money – and the things it can buy – is meant to be owned. It is a mistake of breathtaking proportions to mix up, convolve, confuse or otherwise associate a romantic partner with money. Never do this.

The System gives signals that keep you off balance in this area. The judicial system has a lot of fun making mincemeat out of people who mix their money together, whether romantically involved or not. Marriage is a contract. Divorce is about property rights. When the parties can't agree the judicial system has no way to reconcile emotions. Civil law exists ONLY to sort out property rights (and child custody which is a set of rules having to do with the rights of another human being too young to be held responsible for the mistakes you are teaching him or her to make). The judge does not care who you slept with or if you foolishly answered the question "Does this dress make me look fat?" All the court wants to do is divide up the economic booty. The whoopee is ignored. A judge is just a lawyer who knew a governor. He gets to dress up in robes and sit above clogged courtrooms full of lawyers who did not know a governor. He faces a practical problem. You should know that the NUMBER ONE GOAL of any judge is to get your file off his calendar. He does not care who is right or who is wrong. He does not care who gets custody of the dog. He does not care about justice. He is interested in throughput. The line outside the courthouse is very long and his job is to try to not let it get longer. His desk is LOADED with files. He is in the business of "line 'em up and shoot 'em" and you are just the next target.

So, it is a mistake to mix up money with your romantic partner AND it is a mistake to seek justice from the court system to unwind that mistake. That mistake falls in a special rare category of compound mistakes. Taking a bad decision and making it worse is a curious kind of magic in Mistake-land and nowhere is it easier to accomplish than with romance and money and lawyers.

So, what is one to do? If you are trying to avoid mistakes rather than raise mistake-making to an art form, how does one have a romantic relationship without messing it up with money? Were you not listening, in the prior paragraph? What did I say? "Marriage is a contract" is your clue. The mistake is that people think they must take the one-size-fits-all-two-become-one-what's-yours-is-mine nonsense society dishes out along with wedding planners. WRONG!! You can contract deliberately, delicately and positively in such a way that you and your partner make it clear to each other that neither of you are "in it" for the money. A well-drafted pre-nup is a GIFT to your relationship.

Getting on television

Like Uncle Roger, there is nothing so bad that it can't be made worse by putting it on television. My trophy wife (a bigger prize today than she was more than half a century ago when I met her) and I had a chance to be on The Newlywed Game shortly after we were married but were not chosen. We were lucky to avoid this huge mistake. In the vetting process the producer encouraged everyone to say things that were titillating, risqué or embarrassing. This was during the first Nixon administration when a glimpse of stocking was looked on as something shocking. I am glad no record was made of us under those circumstances. There is still a chance for me to become a Supreme Court Justice and I would not want that fetid mass rolled out at my Senate confirmation hearing.

Today married couples take cellphone videos of themselves doing things that make disgusting look like angel food cake. This is a mistake on an EPIC scale. The fact that it is done AND that other people watch it (can you spell "R-e-a-l-i-t-y T-V"?) is what is known as a Feedback Loop Mistake. It also speaks volumes for what passes for intelligent life on Earth these days.

Other people's spouses

Do I even have to mention this? Apparently so. Here goes. Listen VERY carefully: You may shake the hand of another person's spouse. After knowing another couple a VERY LONG time it is acceptable, in public and fully clothed, to share brief, mutual hugs when arriving and leaving. THAT IS IT!! Jeeeesus, do I have to tell you everything? If you want to make a really HUGE mistake and set off a cascade of other mistakes that demolish everything around you, just violate this rule.

At a more benign level, there is a reality in coupledom which is unavoidable. In every couple, one of them is going to be more gracious, pleasant, engaging and generally enjoyable than the other. To put this on the personal level, it should be no surprise to you by now to hear that all our couple friends eagerly await my wife's arrival while simultaneously grinding their teeth, reminded that she brought me. Deal with it. It is not your fault that your best friend made a mistake.

Children

This is an area where I have no personal experience. We did not have any children. We forgot. We know we are failing to pass on our mistakes and we apologize. We have suffered while our couple friends, initially childless, produced offspring and we did not see them again for 22 years. We have observed, perhaps twice, the inestimable joys of parenthood as children grow, mature and blossom into fare-paying passengers on this bus we call Society. I am sure we are missing a lot and they are not all court appearances.

When your children are the right age (I have NO CLUE when this is) it is a mistake to not sit them down and tell them that you are flawed, you made choices which in retrospect are incredibly foolish, but they were not one of them. Include the tidbit that, knowing what you know now, you have a few moments you would like to re-live. They will be relieved not only to learn that you are human but that you admit it. It warns them that their day to do the same is coming.

Is Marriage a mistake?

Given that my biological parents wandered into a total of eight marriages and one of them produced me, it would seem the answer to this question must be "Yes." On the other hand, some (few?) marriages appear to be successful (definition important here) so maybe we can grant the institution some relief with the answer: "Often but not always." [2]

I find it helpful to start with the most general view, often theoretical. Rather than trying to fix a particular marriage, maybe it is worthwhile to examine The Institution of Marriage itself. Upon close inspection we find that Marriage, as contemplated in Western societies, introduces religion and government into the mix. This results in some interesting, and perhaps fatal, internal conflicts. There are many YouTube videos of animals mating. Watching a few is humbling. Many of these are slightly more humorous than what humans do but essentially not different. All the plumage and makeup are to attract a mate. When choosing from a crowd, animals engage in

---

[2] Two authors have been far more eloquent than I in answering this question. Jerry Klasman's wonderful book <u>Living With Equals</u> and Jim Moran's <u>Why Men Shouldn't Marry</u> should be required reading for anyone contemplating the plunge. Both are long out of print but available – like everything else including a spouse from a foreign country if you want a mistake with an accent – on the internet.

"profiling", something humans have recently made into a dirty word. The seeker asks an "If -then?" question using conditional probability to try to avoid complete randomness. Profiling may have gotten a bad name but everyone does it. Here is a test. The day you got up in the morning and decided it was time for a mate, did you just pick the first candidate you encountered at the bus stop? No, your rule was: "If [other sex or not], then approach." You may have employed compound conditional probability with "If [other sex or not] AND [tall, short, skinny, fat, blonde, brunette, magenta, pick one or more] then approach". Conditional probability is a survival technique whether pairing or choosing between fight or flight. Politicizing it accomplishes nothing.

Rebounding

If divorce is the national pastime, suckering other poor souls into your misery afterwards is the runner-up for things guaranteed to lead to a veritable cacophony of mistakes. There should be a law that condemns divorced people for two years after the split as emotional toxic waste which may not be touched. Imagine having your life subdivided, your children alienated, your finances in disarray and sundry other indignities visited upon you over a period of months or years depending on the acrimony. Do you really think this presents well? And what kind of damaged goods are you likely to find under those conditions? You have now raised mistake making to the fourth power.

Mathematically that works out sort of like this:

(Partner mistake) * (money mistake) * (children mistake) * (divorce mistake) = mistake^4

Congratulations.

How to Make Mistakes

4 - MISTAKES WITH MONEY

This chapter could become a book unto itself. Money is shrouded by myths and shibboleths that defy comprehension. Because money is essentially numeric (Try it: Do you have more if you have a five-dollar bill or a ten-dollar bill?) and because a very large segment of the population is math-phobic, the opportunity for error is boundless.

Making money

Most of us are born poor to one degree or another. Most of us who find that out early in life immediately begin looking around for a way to put a stop to it. There was a time when the solution was simple: If you enjoyed food with your meals you work. No longer. Today more people vote for a living than work for a living. That is sort of an intra-generational "snow-balling" mistake. Not sure where it will end. It is a mistake to believe that someone else will pay for what you want forever. It just won't happen. We may all have to wake up to this one at the same time some day. Occasionally, the aggregate mistakes of humankind over time tip over and instantly translate into Armageddon.[3]

It is a mistake to believe that making money equals success. Lots of people make money, decide they are geniuses and then proceed to lose their money. The net of that is a dual lesson of true intelligence and having no money. People who make money and keep it are financially successful. The mistake is failing to recognize that the "not losing money" business is *different* than the "money making" business. Keeping money means resisting the urge to spend it *and* protecting the principal from gypsies, tramps and thieves determined to take it from you. Not easy.

The Stock Market and the internet are casino operations. Those in charge are very good at probability theory, have large amounts of data on which to base decisions, have big computers and use their skills and data adroitly 24/7 to fleece the unsuspecting. It is a mistake to confuse betting with working. If you luck into some money you should be prepared to luck out of it just as easily. On the other hand, developing a sound ability to work hard and deliver a scarce resource constantly in demand (think: food, housing, medicine) has been a way to make money consistently for centuries. You may

---

[3] For a good time, Google "Complexity Theory, Sand Piles and Financial Crises."

find this works for you, and that you can make and keep money. This does not necessarily make you successful or happy in the general sense. It will just leave you time to hone your non-monetary mistake-making skills.

<u>Keeping money</u>

Once you have money, regardless of how you got it, it is a mistake to think other people will look after it for you. Granted, some will but they will be rare and even then, naturally, will have their own interests at stake. The power of selfishness is not to be under-rated. Harnessing the enlightened self-interest of another person to work for you is a skill worth developing.

Do *not* expect your government to look after your money. Decades ago, P. J. O'Rourke was being charitable when he called Congress a Parliament of Whores.[4] It is a mistake to believe that has changed or that the public has learned anything that will change anything.

The younger generation is in trouble. They want to tweet their way to success. Their mistake is thinking you can acquire and retain money without reading. In the digital age some of the reading is necessarily about mathematics, even less likely anyone under the age of 40 will ever read it. This foretells bad

---

[4] <u>Parliament of Whores: A Lone Humorist Attempts to Explain the Entire U.S. Government</u>, Grove Press, 2003

endings.

Being in business is different than working for a paycheck. Many do not know that. One who choses self-employment needs only four rules:

1. Buy low
2. Sell High
3. Serve your customer
4. Save your money

In a capitalistic economy (disappearing fast but still here on life-support) faithfully observing those rules will pay for all your other mistakes.

Here are some things about money that pegs the mistake-o-meter on High:

1. Buying lottery tickets – the lottery is a tax on people who are bad at math
2. Bernie Madoff
3. Believing tomorrow will be like today
4. Loaning money to friends
5. Confusing betting with working
6. Buying consumption goods and referring to the purchase as "an investment"
7. *Failing* to make prudent insurance purchases (essentially the converse of #1)
8. Being 18 years old or any other age at which you know everything
9. Developing a drug habit or having children who do

10. Borrowing money, especially for consumer purchases, for any reason other than buying an asset with a stream of income sufficient to completely repay the borrowings (this is really a variant of #6 but I needed a list of ten items).

Each of these could be examined in detail. Some are things you should have learned shortly after learning to brush your teeth. The internet is full of material, some terrible, some brilliant. Learning how to separate the two is something that parents and the school system once taught. I am not sure where it is taught today. But knowing how to tell the creeps from the real thing is essential. I can't help you. I am only in the business of describing mistakes, not prescribing cures.

Having written extensively on the subject of investing in many forms over half a century I won't repeat myself. When I was just a boy, I read a good book that offered two simple requirements as fundamental:

1. To accumulate money in any useful amount you must *seriously* want to do it. Saving and investing is not for the faint- or half-hearted;

2. You *must* arrange your life to legally minimize how much of your money goes to the government. This is harder and harder to do each day.

How to Make Mistakes

5 - MISTAKES WITH COMPUTERS

This chapter is about velocity. If you want to make a mistake really fast, use a computer. You can also repeat a mistake very fast over and over again. A good tech mistake that takes only a second can radiate throughout your life and the lives of others over long distances and time periods. Automate your mistakes with Facebook. Post a video on YouTube of yourself playing chess with a goat. The permutations are endless.

Computers help you make mistakes. For instance, a whole generation has grown up using spellcheck with the result that they do not know how to spell. Problem: there are some words (sow, sew, so and vain, vein – there are more) that sound exactly alike but mean very different things. Spellcheck likes them all equally.

Here is how easy it is. Below is the binary

representation of the word "mistake"

0110110101101001011100110111010001100001 0110110101101001011100110111010001100001
10101101100101

And this is the binary representation of the word "misteak"

0110110101101001011100110111010001100101 0110110101101001011100110111010001100101
10000101101011

Copy and paste the second one twelve times and you have made a dozen mistakes. Or have you made a dozen misteaks? See, even a child can do it.

In my teaching days I routinely had lunch at the campus cafeteria. One day I ordered a sandwich and gave the cashier a ten-dollar bill. While waiting at the cash register, I became distracted and did not notice it was taking an inordinate amount of time for the girl to give me my change. When I inquired as to the problem she said "Can you tell me what your change is? The computer screwed up." I answered her while praying she was not registered for one of my classes.

Fake news

While you were sleeping an entire world-wide industry formed for the express purpose of deliberately making mistakes using data. Think of it as a scheme *for inducing you* to make mistakes. It is the reason Sergi Brin and Larry Page have billions of dollars and you are reading this crappy book.

It is called "the internet"

P. T. Barnum said there is a sucker born every minute. But he had to ride around in a wagon and find them one at a time. Sucker production in the digital age has grown to where some fool clicks on the wrong thing every nanosecond. It is a huckster's paradise.

The recipe is simple. Start with a cloud of points like you see below. Using mathematics and probability, find a line that separates Fact from Fiction most of the time (the dotted line in the plot).

All that remains is to manipulate either the data or the mathematics that produced that line or its location, fashioning the snare (solid line) required to trap your prey.

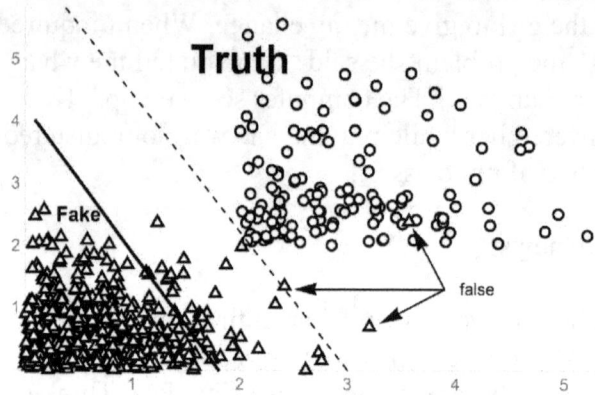

Much of fake news is traceable to errors in the assumptions about data or results. Add to that a mob of journalists who never passed a math class, and you have a 24-hour news cycle that is a Mistake Making Machine wondrous to behold.

Biology

Take computers, a gullible, math-phobic populous and add biology and you are within reach of mistakes that are truly frightening. Click here for Frankenstein:

Introduction to CRISPR-Cas9 | Download the Free eBook Today
Our free CRISPR 101 eBook explains how CRISPR works and helps you get started. Chat Support Available. Comprehensive Guide. Get A Free Trial. Highlights: Experienced Veterans Available, Offering Cost-Effective Research.

One last item

For the two of you left who do not know, it is a mistake to give your bank account number to the widow of the Nigerian Finance Minister who has left thirty-five million dollars in a Swiss bank and needs your authorization to transfer it.

You heard it here first.

How to Make Mistakes

6 - MISTAKES WITH GOVERNMENT

Opportunity is, once again, in great supply here. But we can make sense of it by separating it into categories. One is very general and has to do with how you think about government. The others are transactional and involve dealing with certain governmental agencies and types. We shall explore them separately so you know how you can maximize your mistakes.

Thinking about government

It is a mistake to think you can change government. It is far easier to change yourself. This extends to all sorts of other areas of life, but we will just consider the government component here.

Government exists for a host of different reasons, some benign but most quite pernicious. Starting on the positive, government is necessary for a civil society. It helps us resolve conflicts without too much violence. To this end, government deserves to be supported. I am happy to pay taxes for police, fire protection and an *independent* judiciary as these are services I want and cannot easily provide myself.

Here is a way to employ mistakes to destroy an entire country. It starts with the establishment of the minimum rules for civil order, police and fire protection. Then some people think "Well, that worked out fine, what else can we control?" Thereafter they become enamored with passing all sorts of laws, most of which are mistakes, a few are colossal blunders and still others are some of the stupidest things ever done. Embroil the populous in all manner of social engineering like what sort of bags you may or must use to carry home your groceries, how many kinds of bathrooms you must have and whether you can buy plastic straws. Bad laws lead to mistakes and unintended consequences that ripple through society creating all manner of havoc. When it is realized that a particular law has the precise opposite effect of its announced purpose, rather than just repeal it, another law is passed to "fix" the problem. This is known as compound ripple mistakes, a sort of institutionalized dumb that is really hard to find outside of government. A couple of centuries later, burdened by several hundred thousand misguided and unenforceable laws, all of which are generally ignored by everyone, you have Somalia.

Resisting acknowledgement of error is a special mistake born of arrogance where government really excels. It turns up in the form of keeping things long after the original purpose expired. In Robert Townsend's wonderful book <u>Up the Organization</u> he reports "The British created a civil-service job in 1803 calling for a man to stand on the Cliffs of Dover with a spyglass. He was supposed to ring a bell if he saw Napoleon coming. The job was abolished in 1945"[5]

The mistake is thinking government can, should or will do everything for you. There is a short list of things that government can do. Many people think that list is or should be longer. That is a mistake.

As hordes of well-meaning but lost people, armed with all sorts of conflicting laws and guns, approach with the intent of micro-managing your life to suit their brand of utopia, it is a mistake to think you can overcome that. The natural inclination of government is to expand in the direction of its collapse. This has been proved in many places over centuries. We are just next.

Don't get me started on voting. Everyone has heard the old saying "If you don't vote you can't complain." Nonsense. I don't vote and I am a *world-class complainer of Olympian capabilities.* People think I don't vote because I am above it. Maybe. But my vote is not wasted. I sign my blank vote-by-mail ballot and hand it to my wife. She is

---

[5] Page 60

smarter than I am and as capable as I of choosing between crooks. Besides, if women run things that is fine with me. They could not screw the world up as bad as men have. Women can ill-afford to make mistakes, especially those who are mothers. For decades my advice to young boys has been simple: Always listen to your Father, until he disagrees with your Mother.

So, when it comes to laws, what's a mother to do? Just do what happy people in all other countries do: Ignore them. This brings us to the specifics.

Criminal laws

Laws are generally divided into criminal and civil. It is a mistake to break criminal laws that physically harm another person. Violent criminals must be locked up and government should properly and *only* spend its time doing that.

Then there is a problem with laws regulating so-called "crimes" which do not result in physical harm. Such laws criminalize activities for which there is no victim of violence. Zoning laws are a good example. These laws are all a mistake. Mountains of research proves that land use regulations only employ bureaucrats and move money around between well-connected insiders but do not actually affect long term land use. If you do not believe that, go to Harris County, Texas where the city of Houston may be found. This is 1200 square miles of land mass on which more than four

How to Make Mistakes

million people live very happily without zoning. Their city looks just like yours.

There are many other examples of failed social engineering which criminalize peaceful activity. To list them all would make this book very long. Same with all the wars we have won (The War on Poverty; The War on Inflation; The War on Drugs; The War on Terror, The War on Homelessness; The War on Moping etc.) which are mistakes that lead to all manner of unintended consequences and sad outcomes.[6]

There are other problems. It should be obvious that it is a mistake to shoot your cell phone camera at a police officer while he is shooting his gun at you. But what about shooting your camera at a police officer while he is shooting at someone else? This is a harder question. If that someone else is about to harm you I suspect you will applaud the police officer shooting him. In the other case where your welfare is not involved, does your use of your camera impede the officer in this work? More importantly does it reduce his incentive to do his job? Careful with your answer here, we need police doing the right thing. It is a mistake to trivialize or take lightly these questions. Ponder them and in the unlikely event there is demand for a sequel to this book I will think about it further, too.[7]

---

[6] Watch "The Last Black Man in San Francisco" or the 1977 film "A Piece of the Action" for two excellent if depressing dramatizations.
[7] Working title: "How to Make It Worse"

Civil Laws

This area has to do with commercial activity and (hopefully) non-violent conflict between private parties. Mostly it is about enforcing contracts. Here is a good way to make a mistake in this area. Suppose you have a complex business transaction. You hire a lawyer to write it up. The lawyer went to law school. Your business matter involves economics and finance, therefore mathematics. What you overlook is the fact that your lawyer went to law school *in order to avoid learning math*. Because the lawyer wears a suit and tie and because he sits in an air-conditioned office in a tall building and because he is billing you $1,000 per hour, you think he is a really smart guy. BIG MISTAKE. He may be smart but he knows little about economics and *nothing* about math. Does there exist the occasional quant with a law degree? Sure. But they are as scarce as hen's teeth. You will need a lamp WAY bigger than Diogenes' to find one.

It is a mistake to look for justice in the judicial system. Remember what we said about courts in Chapter 3. Assembly line justice necessarily has a large random component in its outcome. The better thing to do is avoid vexatious people. Don't do business with people who have a history of not performing, of being volatile or having no desire for a reputation for honesty and fair dealing. Suing people is an arduous task. It saps your strength and sours your disposition. There is a lesson in the other direction. You can avoid getting sued by making sure no one gets mad at you. It is a mistake to motivate another party to undertake the distasteful act of initiating a lawsuit which, according to the old Chinese proverb, is a fruit tree planted in the garden of an attorney.

Systems

The central question, pregnant with need for an answer, is: "Who shall decide?" Will choices to be made about your life be determined by you or by some group? This leads to a number of other questions. Here are a few. If not you, who? Who gets to be a member of the group that decides? Who in the group sets the agenda? What are the [actual] motives of those involved? What are the qualifications of the group or anyone in it? Is anyone in the group better suited to make decisions about your life than you are? If so, how did they come by that ability and how did those talents escape you?

Government agencies are interested in power over you. Refusing to surrender to that power can get you branded as an anarchist by some (those who believe decisions should be made by them) or an independent thinker by others (those who believe in individual decision making and personal responsibility). While you may harbor ill-will toward your government and with good reason, it is a mistake not to keep that to yourself.[8] In the meantime, here is a trick you can play on yourself to help cope.

When well-designed (BIG qualification here), all systems seek optimal outcomes *on average*. What you encounter in government and what causes you frustration is the fact that you are not average. You are an individual and have individual characteristics the system does not have programmed into it. It is a mistake to view this as a fatal flaw regardless of how it may seem or actually be. Better that you adjust your attitude and work with the system to bend it ever so slightly in your direction with good humor and persistence. The alternative is life-threatening. It is a mistake to die over a government action. Unfortunately, in the name of defending our country many have done so. This conundrum does not yield to easy explanation.

Natural Laws

So we know that lawyers go to law school to avoid learning Mathematics. The best way to get a lawyer to check his cell phone is to use the M word in his presence. Lawyers are fascinated with passing laws they *think* will control people's behavior. This is a mistake and the proof is in how few people modify their behavior because of laws passed by others.

---

[8] I know this casts a question on the entire enterprise of writing this book. Think of it as "do as I say, not as I do."

There is an old saying in the practice of law: If the facts are against you argue the law; if the law is against you argue the facts. This, a clue in itself, highlights the reality that the law and the facts are often in conflict with one another. To make this point clearer here is an example where the facts and the law are in almost perfect agreement. Compare this law: $F = G \frac{m^1 m^2}{r^2}$ with the one on this sign

The equation is the law of gravity; the drawing depicts the facts. The outcome is the same regardless. The reason this is true is that *gravity is a Law of Nature*. No amount of passing laws of men will overcome this. You can't repeal stupid.[9]

---

[9] See "Indiana Pi Bill" in Wikipedia for a famous example of legislative stupidity in this area.

Government and religion

Our founding fathers were brilliant. They made very few mistakes. One of their best moves was to keep government and religion separate. Here is a pictorial explanation of why they thought that was a good idea.

The Founders came from a place where government and religion were literally across the street from each other for centuries. They thought this was a bit too chummy. It is useful to categorize groups who want to decide for you into two classes, government and religion. Each of these groups are certain they know more about what you should be doing than you do. In the heart of London, over just a few blocks, a handful of buildings contain multitudes of tiny tyrants of one flavor or the other. Our Founders thought it a mistake to allow these two types to mingle.

Bully for them.

7 - MISTAKES WITH REAL ESTATE

Somewhere it is written that "Under all is the Land." It may be that the land is all that matters. All wars are nominally about religion but actually about land. The players may be talking about The Lord but they are keeping score in the land.

Since many of us are crowded into urban areas and real estate is roughly divided into "unimproved" and "improved" it is reasonable to create mistake categories along the same lines.

<u>Mistakes with land</u>

The land is a resource for human use. Using it wisely is a kind of art. Many are eager to tell you how you may use your land for it gives them a feeling of great power. Verily, these are known as Hysterical Environmentalists. It is a mistake to become one of them. Ultimately, if you do, you find that what you are really doing is asking others to conserve resources so that those resources are available to you. What gives you the right to tell people who live in Africa that they cannot have a refrigerator when you do?

One should still be a wise steward of the land. Fouling the water that passes over your land is a mistake as your downstream neighbor should receive water as clean as you did.

The argument that we should save the land "for our children" is hollow. If true, that should also apply to the children who should then save the land for their children, who then should save it for their children…ad infinitum. In the limit this means that no land should ever be used for anything, which is nonsense. Are the dolphins trying to save YOU? On the other hand, it is a mistake to think that the land will support an unlimited number of people. True Environmentalists are those who choose to limit their output of new people. Their carbon footprint is, by definition, smaller because they added fewer new feet to the planet.

There are pieces of land that are improved but have no buildings on them. These are called golf courses. Golf is a sport where you excel by hitting the ball the least. Hence, a champion would not hit it at all. It is a mistake to hit a ball and then *you* go and get it. Draw your own conclusions.

Mistakes with real estate can be serious and long

lasting, affecting a lot of people. The US is a highly developed society with an elaborate set of rules that have stood the test of time. In other countries where care of the land is ignored or laws are ignored, wide swaths of land can be left unusable for years after the mistakes.

Mistakes with buildings

Here we have a giant collection of mistake categories. You can build the wrong building or build it in the wrong place or at the wrong time or with the wrong financing. Or, you can build it badly. The term "construction mistake" is redundant since the main task of a contractor is to screw up.

When I was very young and new in the business, I offered a rental house for sale that, so I said, was zoned for two dwellings. Trouble was the zoning line was in the middle of the street that passed in front of the property. I had held the plat map upside down when determining the zoning for my parcel. The multi-family zoning was, in fact, across the street from the property I was selling. That mistake was very costly and I promised myself never to make it again. Years later when investigating a loan on a newly constructed house I noticed the driveway connected to the lot line on the other side of the house from where the access easement to the parcel was located. The driveway was thus constructed on the wrong side of the land. And the garage the driveway serviced was on the wrong side of the house. The pavement was on a part of the land the owner had no right to pass over. This was a mistake made with a lot of help. The owner, architect, builder, permitting authority and all the inspectors had gone through the whole procedure with the plat map held upside down. I was really proud of them. I realized this mistake is one that persists through time. Once I pointed it out the error A LOT OF PEOPLE had to go back and do a lot of things. Genius is the ability to evade work by doing something right the first time.[10]

---

[10] This line is not mine. I have heard and repeated it my entire life. Now, with the Ninnernet I thought I might be able to find a proper attribution. A web search credits "American Salesman" whatever that is. A variant is attributed to Elbert Hubbard, whoever he is.

Mistakes with real estate and government

I once heard that 80% of the decisions made by the San Diego City Council were land use decisions. Knowing that a huge portion of government actions are mistakes makes this statistic rather sobering. According to Google, the area of San Diego is 372 square miles.[11] As of 2017 the population of the city was estimated to be 1.42 million. Ignoring the sides of cliffs, riverbeds and some deserts area which are inhabitable, that is a little more than 7300 square feet per person. Sound crowded? That is because it is.

Residents of Wyoming have more than 4.7 *million* square feet.

Each.

---

[11] The same Google page also says the Area Code is 619 when there are actually three telephone area codes in San Diego county, at least two of which are in the City of San Diego. Have I told you yet that everything you read on the internet is true?

How to Make Mistakes

8 - MISTAKES WITH EDUCATION

School *should* be the place where you learn to avoid mistakes. After all, there are only a few things that work *all the time* and those are the things one should learn in school.

If only it were true.

<u>Never do this!</u>

When I was in graduate school my least inspiring professor once said that the Theory of College Education was: You teach undergraduates to answer the question "What is?" You teach Masters students to answer the question "How to?" And PhD students are supposed to answer the question "Why?" This struck me at the time as a passel of wrong-headed bunk. I have asked "Why?" all my life. People should be encouraged to ask that question from the instant they enter this screwed up world starting with: "Why am I attached to this woman?" "Why?" is the polite version of questioning authority. It is the underlying reason free speech is so important.[12]

I remember walking with that same professor across the Penn State Campus 25 years ago. I had gone back to graduate school in my late 40s with the romantic and lofty goal of changing the world one student at a time. This professor was one of the most cynical and unhappy people I have ever known. By my second year those in my department who were paying attention had learned two things about me. One was that I was a zealot on a mission; the other was that my time of life had delivered me into their midst with debating skills that far exceeded the usual 25-year-old PhD student they were in the habit of intimidating.

When I entered Penn State in 1995 the University's annual budget was $1.4 billion, an amount greater than the GDP of many countries. I do not remember the subject the professor and I were arguing about, but I was pressing my position in my usual relentless way. Perhaps because I was gaining ground, perhaps because this professor wanted none of my argument, he stopped our walk, turned to me and said something I have never forgotten: "Listen! Do you think you are going to change anything? Look around you." He gestured with a grand wave

---

[12] We are all indebted to Ilan Samson for reinforcing the importance of the question "Why?" in his wonderful book Demathtifying: Demystifying Mathematics.

of his arm at the surrounding behemoth that is the PSU main campus. "All of this is built up, maintained and arrayed about us to keep people like you from changing anything."

My bubble burst. It was then I realized that my nascent theory about "systems" which boils down to "If you want health stay out of the health care system" and "if you want justice stay out of the judicial system" included the education system.

School as a Mistake Making Machine

Like many things in modern life, the academy has been turned on its head. Thanks to politics, today school has little to do with education and mostly to do with indoctrination. Just by watching the system in action one can easily conclude that if you want to learn something, the last thing you do is enroll in school.

How can this be? How is it that mistake-making has replaced mistake-avoidance as the primary subject taught in school? Actually, there is a nice equation that draws on a simple reality: Whenever you introduce politics into a system you reduce the output of the system. Suppose that A = Academia, a pure and good thing that promotes teaching and learning and Mr. Chips, extolling the value of knowledge and reason above all else. Now define E = Education and P = Politics, then:

$$E = A + P$$

where "P" is always a negative number. This should make the point quite nicely. So, reality is:

$$E = A + (-P) = A - P$$

E is therefore always smaller than A. Eventually, which is the case we have today, the absolute value of P is greater than the value of A. Result: E becomes negative.

It is a mistake to believe otherwise.

Teachers

The mistake teachers most often make is forgetting the *first rule of customer satisfaction* which is: you must care about what happens to your students. An example of a terrible mistake is someone teaching who hates to teach.

Great teachers are a treasure. Some are remembered for all the best reasons long after their students have graduated. It is a mistake to undervalue these people. But we do.

People often ask me if I am an engineer, which is an insult to engineers but that is another story. I always respond by saying "No, but I had a great high school geometry teacher." I use something he taught me every day. He was not alone. I was blessed by great math teachers all through my education who not only taught me to ask "Why?" but to measure the answer precisely.

Unions

An entire chapter could be devoted to this and expanded well beyond education. But, for all the damage done by Unions in every walk of life, it is particularly terrible in education. Take the equation above and modify it as follows:

$$E = A + P^U$$

where all the definitions are the same and U is a very large uneven number.[13] The result of this is to make the final value of E less than zero *much sooner*. The City of New York has a place called a "rubber room" (Google it) that are actually "centers" that hold hundreds of teachers who have been deemed unfit to be in contact with students (let your imagination run wild on this one). Nonetheless, protected by their union, they sit all day doing nothing and drawing full pay. Your tax dollars [not] at work.

Then there is tenure, a form of cancer. I have 3 graduate school credits with the grade "A" on my transcript for a class that never convened because the tenured professor never showed up for class. Ever. It was an open secret that this was taking place, but it was never discussed. It taught a great lesson to students eager to become professors and

---

[13] If you do not know why it must be uneven you missed a math class.

never again be held accountable. What those young, impressionable minds overlooked was that, once their own tenure was achieved, they would never again be taken seriously.

Tenure is lifetime employment without the possibility of parole.

9 - MISTAKES WITH HEALTH

Since making mistakes with your health can be fatal, this chapter probably should have been first. That way if you are spectacularly successful at screwing up early in life you might be spared making many more mistakes just by starting out here.

The FUNDAMENTAL ERROR in the whole Health Care Kerfuffle is ignoring, overlooking or failing to admit one simple fact: The person most interested in your health is YOU. Until you recognize and accept this reality there is very little that will improve your health. Your doctor, overworked, underpaid, hopefully caring, (even more hopefully) competent soul that he is, stands as a *distant* second to you as a defense against poor health. Believing that some lying charlatan, of any political stripe, on television trying to get elected cares about your health is akin to believing in the

Tooth Fairy. Period. Ask your doctor about Medicare for All. He's not a bit worried. He knows that Nature's Laws will send the same number of unlucky souls to parade naked before him regardless of the laws of man or any campaign slogan.

Here is a simple rule: The farther someone is from your skin, the less that person cares about your health.

In his very informative and enjoyable book, <u>The Future of Everything</u>, David Orrell describes mankind's obsession with prediction. He concentrates on three areas of modern life: Health, Finance and the Weather.

The news is not good.

It turns out that when meteorologists feed last week's data into today's forecasting model, they can't predict *yesterday's* weather. Results of following the recommendations of so-called "professional financial advisors" vary little from what you would get if you trained monkeys to throw darts at a stock page taped to the wall. Predicting health outcomes is only slightly better. But it is better since barbers stopped practicing medicine and became stockbrokers. Simply, the science of medicine has improved over the years as snake oil salesmen have moved into finance.
But it is not always a mistake to consult a physician. Rare events and obscure diseases do happen. Most

of good health and longevity comes from three things that have little to do with your buddy in the white coat: genetics, diet and exercise. The first you can't do much about other than confirming your actual donors (your mother will be less in doubt). The other two are just a matter of discipline.

Therefore, it is a mistake to weigh 100 pounds more than your parents combined. It *can* be a mistake to go to a doctor unless you have debilitating pain as a result of being hit by a large object.

My great-grandfather once described doctors as "educated guessers." This was not meant to be a compliment but actually was. The best doctor has seen a lot of cases like yours. From that experience, together with a good understanding of the probabilistic aspects of biology, he *might* be able to make a guess more educated than yours.

The key is to find "the best doctor" which gets harder with passing years. I am at the age where finding a doctor older than I am is unlikely. Having someone a third my age digitally massaging tender parts of my cute little body is worrisome. What I worry about is the probability that he has seen fewer cases of Mogo on the Gogo than I have.

Perhaps the most persistent mistake made in medicine is one that, when made, benefits pharmaceutical companies (why are we not surprised?) The mistake is reporting probability of improvement as a relative number. The better way is to report using absolute numbers.[14] The sound you hear of Big Pharma picking your pocket is: "Studies show a 50% improvement after taking Gogoistan." It may be true that the control group had two cases of Mogo on the Gogo and the experimental group taking Gogoistan had only one. Yes, 1% is 50% of 2%. True, but misleading, especially when a stressful decision about your health is involved.

Suppose your doctor told you

(a) This drug has proven to reduce symptoms by 50%; or
(b) Out of every 100 people, two will have these symptoms but if they all take this drug only one will have them.

Both statements are true. Which statement is more likely to persuade you to take the drug? What is left out of the first statement is the crucial fact that out of every 100 people, 98 are never going to have the problem in the first place.

It turns out that humans understand absolute numbers (simple, positive, whole integers like 1, 2, 3,...,100) far better than relative numbers (percentages). There is also an easy metric that provides a proper context by portraying results in scale. It is called Numbers Needed to Treat (NNT). This is (sort of) the answer to the question: How

---

[14] An excellent book on this is Calculated Risks by Gerd Gigerenzer (2002)

many must be involved before a noticeable difference is detected? In modern industrial societies, most diseases are rare at young ages. The fear factor, however, is overstated when the risk is expressed in relative numbers. NNT helps overcome that.

There is a famous example used in Stat 101 that illustrates this. It is called the False Positive Paradox which is a special case of the Base Rate Fallacy. Both of these are easily researched on the Web. If you are planning to get sick it is a mistake not to read up on these before talking to a doctor. Your doctor REALLY likes to hear you start a sentence with "I read on the internet…"

Another huge mistake is to conflate health care and insurance. Nature does not care if you are covered. If your body is going to be invaded by a noxious bug, that critter does not check your insurance first. Your insurance company does not provide good health. It provides (some) money to pay for (some) health interventions. That is it, nothing more. The idea that your insurance company cares about your health is as silly as expecting the government to care about you. All insurance companies are in the *business* of collecting premiums and *not* paying claims. This is not an indictment of insurance companies. We need insurance companies and the way they stay in business, like all businesses, is to take in more revenue (premiums) than they pay out in costs (claims). Deal with it.

I once heard a cardiologist say he retired because he had grown weary of spending 10 hours a day telling people to lose weight and stop smoking. So, in the end, until you form a close relationship with an exercise bicycle, resolve to swim three days a week or get up off the couch and walk a mile a day you are doomed. If you seek out fresh fruit and green, leafy vegetables daily, dial back the carbohydrate intake and don't put burning leaves in your mouth you have a chance. If you don't want to do any of those things stop reading this now, put the book down and go have another bag of Doritos. I don't care.

Also, I would stay off skateboards.

10 - MISTAKES WITH CLIMATE

If you think about it (which is what I would like you to do), the title of this chapter is silly. How does someone make mistakes *with* climate? For the moment lets imagine that you can.

Making mistakes *about* climate used to be hard. Charles Dudley Warner (or Mark Twain or someone else, who knows?) once said "Everybody complains about the weather, but nobody does anything about it." The same is true today, there are just more people talking about it and communication technology has amplified their voices. But the number of people doing something about it is the same: zero.

Did people worry about the ice age? If an ice age were to occur now you can bet the internet would make it colder. They say an asteroid struck the earth millions of years ago and wiped out all of life.

Perhaps not all, because something had to remain to lead to us. But somehow, I can't see those dinosaurs worrying about it. I am such a dinosaur for my time and you can be, too.

Concern vs. Worry

It is a mistake to worry about things you can do nothing about. This leads to a definitional issue. We need to agree that "concern" is a useful activity which has to do with things you can influence such as your health, your personal finances, your driving habits, etc. On the other hand, "worry" is an unproductive activity when the subject is something you cannot affect. You should be concerned about your children's education and encourage them to complete their homework and respect their teachers because you can *reach* your children. There is a host of other things out of reach, the climate being one, that it is useless to worry about.

There are at least three distinct questions involved in the so-called "climate science" debate: 1) Is the planet warming? Let's say "yes" on this one; 2) is the warming caused by human activity? It seems reasonable that more than seven billion people produce more of everything, including climate changing (warming?) activities than, say, the four billion people crowding the planet in 1974. So, we will give that one a "yes" also; 3) Is there anything you can do about it? Only human arrogance can produce a "yes" for this one.

Scale

Human beings overestimate their ability to influence Nature. Mostly this is about misunderstanding scale. Take, for example, travel safety. It is widely known that air travel is a lot safer than automobile travel. The reason could be that pilots are better drivers or planes are better engineered. Even if this is true, there is a far better, easier explanation related to the scale of the space in which each mode of transportation operates. Imagine the navigable roadways not as surfaces but of very long, often intersecting, square tubes which are, on average, about 60 feet wide and 15 feet tall. Now consider the volume of those tubes through which millions of vehicles must pass. Using only the United States Interstate Highway System's 46,876 miles, the volume of all those tubes is about 223 billion cubic feet. Now consider air travel over the same area. Planes do not have to stay in their lane. The only similarity of their path to that of cars is neither may pass underground or under water. You should be getting the drift here. If a car must pass through a tube about 15 feet high, a plane has a path that is *waaaayyyy* higher. Let's say the average commercial airplane flies at, again on average, 35,000 feet. That is 2,333 times more *vertical* space than the height devoted to surface traffic. Now go laterally. The 48 contiguous states of the U. S. cover an area of more than 3 million square miles. The numbers start to get very large here so let's give me credit for being able to use a calculator and just say that the volume of air over the United State is *a lot*.

In fact, just comparing (1) the airspace over US Interstate Highway System to a height of 15 feet to (2) the total air space over the continental US to a height of 35,000 feet, planes have more than *13 million times more space to occupy than cars.* So the main reason air travel is so safe is that is very hard for an airplane to find another airplane to bump into. All of this is *without* considering the number of moving objects in each space. Think of how many people you know who own cars compared to how many people you know who own airplanes.

When talking about climate we are dealing with a volume not constrained by national boundaries or land masses or commercial air travel. Remember you have the same number of nitwits walking, driving and flying around as you have breathing air. That available air is *waaaayyyy, waaaayyyy* more than the volume we were just discussing.

Here is a way to think of the puny influence man has on his environment.[15] Consider a large room – 20 feet by 20 feet, 10 feet tall. Imagine one wanted to burn something that would create in this 4,000 cubic foot volume, *proportionally*, the same CO_2 emission that all the private cars in the world belch into the atmosphere during a whole year. Thus, we are trying to produce the same

---

[15] This is another gem from Ilan Samson. But it is controversial. Others dispute this argument. Someone has made a mistake.

additional *concentration* of CO_2 by human activity.[16]

Performing this experiment, you can compound your mistake by accidentally burning down your house. To avoid this let's not burn gasoline, but use matches instead. How many matches would have to be burned in total over the whole year, to (proportionally) inflict on the atmosphere of this room what all the world's cars do to the earth's atmosphere in a year?

You start not with matches but a scalpel. Then, take one match and carefully chop it up into *twenty* bits of equal length. Nineteen of them can be thrown away - not needed. You are left with one remaining tiny sliver: If one burns this *once in the whole year* the room will have been treated to what, proportionally, all the world's cars do to the Earth's atmosphere each year.

The next time Earth Day rolls around, be sure to tell the Earth to "Have a Nice Day!" It will.

An Even Bigger Risk

From all of this comes one certainty: You can *always* count on being plagued by fear mongering pretenders to the throne trying to extract votes from a gullible populace. Threats of climate change are just the latest in a long list of things politicians use

---

[16] Admittedly just *one* human activity, but just go with me for the moment.

to whip the public into a frenzy in the hope they can get into office and pass laws to take control of other people's lives, all while collecting large, risk-free salaries and pensions. In fact, the whole of campaigning reduces to discovering the right fear and fanning its flames in the days immediately prior to an election.[17]

Passing laws to regulate human behavior is a fool's errand. People will seek that which furthers their best interests, regardless of laws of men prohibiting the same.[18] The laws of men are something the Universe gives humans to play with while waiting for Nature to act.

Should you be a good citizen of the world, a conscientious guardian of the land? Yes, because it makes you feel good to do so. There is no altruism.[19] Everyone is selfish, only some of us admit it.

The great averaging machine of life will control those things you worry about. Free yourself of this, go forth and live. Nature thins the herd when necessary and won't ask your permission. Whether

---

[17] H. L. Menchen said it best in his 1918 book In Defense of Women "The whole aim of practical politics is to keep the populace alarmed (and hence clamorous to be led to safety) by an endless series of hobgoblins, most of them imaginary."

[18] See Robert Lucas, Jr. 1995 Nobel Prize in Economics for confirmation.

[19] See short, tragic life of mathematical biologist George R. Price who worried about something he could do nothing about.

it is global warming, a good pandemic or nuclear war, put your money on Nature. Come to think of it, maybe that is what politicians are for, making giant blunders which cancel each other out. A nuclear winter should resolve the warming climate problem.

Many terrible things can happen. Remember three things about this. One is that just because it happened does not mean you caused it. Two is, that no matter who caused it, politicians rarely have the answer. Finally, and most importantly for your own peace of mind, people tend to miscalculate which ones are really important.

A Prediction

While you are worrying, think about what would happen if California had an atomic weapon. It would declare war on Texas. California is The Green New Deal on steroids. Before long I expect a law declaring the use of plastic straws in California to be a capital offense. Eventually California will realize that people in Texas are able to use their backyard barbeques any time they want, drive cars powered by petroleum, and worse, they are allowed to keep a substantial portion of the money they earn.

California is a place where *everyone knows better than everyone else what someone else should be doing.* Once they see millions of people in Texas living their own lives without interference there can only be one outcome: **SECTARIAN VIOLENCE!!**

Watch for it. Soon California will be arming their homeless and sending them to other states to enforce the kind of righteousness that only Californians have in sufficient quantity to share.

Another first for this book. You'll have to admit you can't get these kinds of insights just anywhere.

11 - MISTAKES WITH AGING

It is a mistake to become a Grumpy Old Man. Avoid it if you can. Your family will thank you for it. But it is not easy. When I was a lot younger, I resolved never to begin a sentence "Kids, these days…" Now about every second sentence I utter starts with those words.

Time Passes

There comes a time when you realize that the mid-life crisis you had in your mid-life was for a good reason. Something new hurts every week. Suddenly you realize that the words "…so I can spend more time with my family…" is code for someone being sick. Clients who were, like you, in their 20s when you met now have *grandchildren* heading off to college.

You attend a lot of funerals.

These are all signposts reading "You are not a kid anymore" or "Caution – The End is Near." So what should you/can you do about it?

If you are lucky and have one that has put up with you all these years, listen to your wife. It is long overdue, she is probably aging far more gracefully than you are and she has always been smarter than you are.[20]

Fear not, you still have time to make some big mistakes. The short list would include trying to hang on to your job longer than you should, trying to prevent all manner of change, ignoring your family and those around you who, despite your being a Class One Idiot, care about you.

Here is a trick that is not so much an antidote but a way to think about the problem. Recognize that challenge keeps you alive and involved. On the other hand, stress will kill you. Make three lists:

1. Things you won't do (these probably have been around for a while and define who you are)
2. Things you should not do (like get on ladders)
3. Things you can't do (you know what is on this list, if you can remember)

---

[20] This sentiment is part of another wonderful out of print book, <u>Brown's Guide to Growing Gray</u> by David Brown (no relation). I keep a copy on my desk.

Aging is about judiciously moving items between these lists such that you find the line between challenge and stress. The line is a moving target but you need to remain on the correct side of it. Doing this is a delicate process, about as easy as tap dancing in a canoe, but critical.

The earlier chapter with my rant about health gets a redux here. Your doctor is now dead and to replace him you have only youngsters to choose from out of a pool of "Kids these days…" This can be a good thing if he/she/it/they/ze/hir went to a good school *and* actually attended class. It is a mistake to look at it otherwise because, like much of your remaining miserable life, YOU HAVE NO CHOICE!!! It is a mistake to fight these realities.

<u>Age and Money</u>

Getting older with a little money is better than the alternative. Here are a few things you need to ensure the mistakes you made in Chapter 4 are truly life changing.

There is a recurrent theme in this book, if indeed it has any coherent structure at all, relating to *systems*. The foundation of a good system includes some unavoidable mathematics. Here is something approximating the mathematical concept of a recurrence relation.[21]

---

[21] Maybe it is an infinite regress. I am torturing the math all through here so why stop now?

Every day is a lifetime for someone in their 90s…
Every week is a lifetime for someone in their 80s…
Every month is a lifetime for someone in their 70s…

Are you picking up the trend? Find your decade. Or, run it down to small numbers and you will understand why teenagers think they are immortal.

Good luck with that.

Reality is the system illustrated by the following mortality plot. The bottom axis is your age. The left axis is the probability you will live another year. The large white space on the left is the part of your life you have squandered up to age 70. The gray area is what everyone 70 years old have, on average, remaining. If you have not spent all your money and if you have kept your savings away from your government, you have an Individual Retirement Account, company savings plan or the equivalent. Current tax law requires you to take a required minimum distribution (RMD) each year beginning at age 70. That amount is a percentage of your savings, rising each year, shown on the right axis. Neither your government nor you should be worried about anything after age 100.[22] Basically,

---

[22] Only the mortality table cares about these things. Depending on your genetics and health you may not be interested in some other age prior to 100.

your small, remaining life is in that circle on the plot. Don't spend it all in one place.

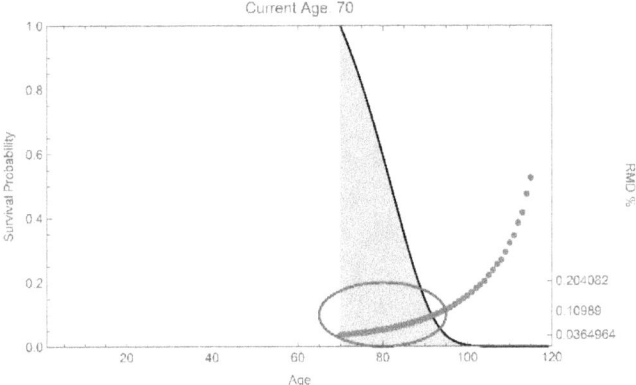

One last thing. If you are planning on getting older, have a daughter.

How to Make Mistakes

12 - MISTAKES WITH RELIGION

It is a mistake to make fun of someone else's religious beliefs. Not just because you come off as a jerk but also because there is an even chance that they are right, and you are wrong. This is a delicate subject that requires careful handling. People hold all sorts of beliefs and most deserve respect.[23]

More than once I have been encouraged to think about God by people who I respect and care about. Given the fact that each day I grow ever closer to finding out, naturally I have given the matter more careful thought recently. I have spent an adult lifetime paying more attention to secular things than metaphysical. During those years it has been comforting to deal with and believe in things I could touch. As I move closer to the day when I will

---

[23] The qualification "most" is to rule out those extremes and fringes that involve violence which has no place anywhere, regardless of how justified.

no longer touch anything but the inside of a coffin, it is natural to renew my inquiry into what comes next. Along the way, I found an idea to provide cover for my more devout friends, not that they need it or asked me for it.

Religion and Science

The last chapter of this effort, next following, confirms what the reader may have already surmised, that I am a soul-less numbers cruncher who views most of life through a haze of probabilistic calculations. My world view is heavily influenced by that tiny part of science I barely understand.

My last round of education, undertaken when nearing 50 years of age, introduced further introspection into the nature of the transcendental. Encounters with Blaise Pascal and Rev. Bayes were stimulating. Science necessarily depends on mathematics. The foundation of mathematics in turn rests on proof. Underlying proof is evidence. Trace the foregoing line of reasoning backwards and believing in God becomes a stretch, or so I thought until recently. From nearly every angle it appears to the casual observer that believers and non-believers alike have the same amount of evidence, either all of it or none of it depending on your perspective. To a puzzle solver, which is how I like to think of myself, this makes the question of whether there is a God uninteresting. Puzzles get solved when it is possible to gather and rely on a preponderance of evidence on a particular side. Such a dominance tips the scales in one direction or another. Resolution is satisfying. My view has always been that atheism is a faith-based religion as much as any other.

So, it is not a mistake to live happily in the middle. Grant people their beliefs and reserve judgment on who is right until such time as you see evidence sufficient to lead you to proof in an acceptable form. If there is a forgiving God, pray that he will forgive you for waiting until you meet to decide.

Quants Only Think They Know

Rather than arguing over which miracle is least likely, maybe another approach is required. It is perhaps time to re-think things in the digital age because disruption of thought is carried on in so many ways everywhere in the ether every day. Doing so we strip some of the smugness from the quants. Mathematicians should be careful throwing stones. Many "proofs" rely on limit theorems, essentially an assumption about what happens as the number of observations, n, approaches a particular point. Often that point is Infinity. As far as I know we have no mathematicians returning from Infinity to report the news about Infinityland any more than we have any recent resurrections. Infinity is a convenient mathematical construct that permits proofs to be written down. Underlying that activity is the BELIEF that Infinity exists and that it exists in a form consistent with a particular argument.

Then there is the matter of the mathematical definition of "the limit" which is a place near Infinity you can never get to. Sounds suspiciously like Heaven to me.

Consider this dilemma: If n counts the number of observations, n at Infinity means that we have full and complete information, all the facts are in, there is no uncertainty. Since many mathematical proofs work to advance probability theory, one wonders if anyone has noticed an apparent contradiction. Infinity is the place where the least probable thing MUST happen, all uncertainty is resolved. With no uncertainty why does one need a theory of probability? Do we still need God at that stage? If God exists, then by the time we reach Infinity shouldn't we have seen him or her by then? If we haven't does that mean there is no God or there is no Infinity?

Careful with the rejoinder: "Infinity is not a place, it is an abstract concept." Far as I can tell, so is God. Also, exercise caution when claiming that mathematics with its reliance on Infinity has sent a vehicle to Mars. Perhaps, but Mars is still far short of Infinity.

Mathematicians have an Imaginary Number. Go Figure. Don't even get me started on dividing by zero. C'mon: "Undefined"? Really? How can people with that position criticize those whose preferred deity is, for them, only visible in the distant fog but still visible?

It helps to separate faith from religion for the same reason it is good to separate academia from education. In both cases the former is the (more or less) pure concept in its best light. The latter is the politicized version of the ideal corrupted by predators and tenure. Give me all the faith and academics and the Universe is a better place; you can keep the religious and education establishments as dens iniquity boiling the pot of human trouble ever faster.

Pascal had it right. Evaluating the ***risk*** of being wrong on the subject of God is worth doing and leads to a solution (albeit including the ever-ephemeral and elusive Infinity). Rev. Bayes not so much. His Degree of Belief approach finds purchase in the secular world more and more as Big Data engulfs us. The stretch to faith is still just that - a stretch - for math or religion.

There is a wonderful set of electronic objects in various places on the internet (start with Wikipedia - which moves closer to God each day) titled "Powers of Ten" and similar variants. The original 1977 version (https://youtu.be/0fKBhvDjuy0) on YouTube makes a pretty good point about where we fit into the Universe, whether the physical universe or the universe of belief systems (perhaps the same?)

You can raise a number to the power of infinity and, depending on the number you start with, you will get something either infinitely large or infinitely small. Can you raise a number to the Power of God?

Maybe mathematics is also a faith-based religion...

13 - A CASE STUDY IN MISTAKES

[Spoiler Alert: The Geeks are going to win]

Here is where we are now. You can ignore government. You can ignore religion. But apparently you cannot ignore your cellphone. Let's address the mistake you make when you slavishly follow armies of clever, nation-less programmers intent on modifying your behavior. You may not be able to avoid it, but we proceed on the premise that it would be at least a little bit useful to know something about how the geeks do it.

Or not.

Now that you know how to make mistakes in various areas and how you can compound those mistakes by artfully mixing and matching, we put it all together. In this chapter we will examine what happens when mistakes are made involving people, government, Nigerian scammers and computers all at the same time. We will explore how the cascade of interwoven mistakes affects our daily lives, making the clusterf**k World we live in seem like a Swiss watch. Indeed, with the internet as a mistake delivery system, unless we live in a cave, it is impossible to avoid being buried by mistakes.

The question

Suppose we wonder if human beings are animals. This is an unresolved question in many fields. It is also very broad. It is a mistake to think that everyone in the World but you, refined, pleasant, delicate soul that you are, is an animal. This is a mistake because everyone else thinks of themselves as delightful and respectful, making you part of the animal population from their perspective. What we must do is (a) narrow the question; and (b) eliminate subjective bias. It is a mistake to think doing either of these things is easy to do.

A subset

Biologists agree that human beings are animals. They might be a little more careful and describe us as mammals. We are warm blooded if not always warm hearted. We are vertebrates who are sometimes spineless. We are, if lucky, born live. Even biologists must deal with exceptions. To narrow the question, we ignore distinguishing physical characteristics and, offending anthropologists,[24] concentrate on behavioral differences between animals and humans. We will ask if humans *act like* animals without spending too much time thinking about whether we must omit rugby players from the database.

The bias problem

To at least start on eliminating bias, we could collect some data. Data is supposed to objectify matters, substituting the anonymity of numbers for YOU. This can be done in a variety of ways. One is to take surveys, asking people what they think. If you believe in this mythology, test it with a simple a one-question survey "True or False: All men are jerks?" Get a bunch of clipboards and set up your card table outside the ladies restroom in any bus station.

It is a mistake to expect people to tell you the truth.[25]

Having lived long enough to doubt my fellow man, I believe that watching what people do rather than listening to what they say produces better data. So, let's do that.

---

[24] Cf. Horace Mitchell Miner, "Body Ritual Among the Nacirema," *American Anthropologist*, 58(3), pp. 503-07, June, 1956.

[25] This is where I begin to get into trouble with a lot of researchers who have built their careers on survey data. To those people I say: Get a life. Yes, I know there are methods to control for such things and improve your shot at getting honesty from survey participants. If I had wanted to write a statistics textbook, I would have written a statistics textbook.

Further narrowing has us asking what sort of human activity tends in the direction of animal behavior. An easy choice is criminal behavior. Surely criminals are animals. Really? What about the clergyman who gets a traffic ticket for making an illegal right turn? Fine, we will restrict our inquiry to violent crimes. Fortunately, there are a relatively few people who commit crimes of violence against their fellow humans. But are these people anything but aberrations? We just said we have heartless and spineless humans who still qualify as people. It takes all sorts to make a World and what we have here is a World.

It is a mistake to make generalizations.[26] But it is necessary to generalize in order to fashion rules about what constitutes a civil society. So, we can avoid a mistake by recognizing the limits of data analysis. Whatever "evidence" our data delivers, the conclusion we reach from it will *always* be subject to exceptions. This is known as uncertainty. It is a mistake to believe that we can eliminate all uncertainty. Also, data analysis seeks a prediction of some sort of middle, often average, value. This, as pointed out in the earlier chapter about government, is unsatisfying to those who view themselves as exceptional.

---

[26] The alert reader will recognize this sentence as a generalization.

For now, we will ***assume*** [27] that people who commit violent crimes represent an *extreme* exception to normal human behavior and that studying that subset of humanity will lead us to useful information about whether there is a difference between humans and animals.

One last tweak

There have been many studies of how Nature deals with over-crowding. The term "thinning the herd" is, for some, a white-hot buzzword. Others will object to characterizing criminal behavior as animal behavior. Rather than get carried away in sea of political correctness, we will frame our most general question as follows: Is there a detectable spatial relationship in criminology? Stated differently, we are interested in whether crime increases with increased population given a constant habitable land mass. Thus, finally, our empirical question becomes: Does violent crime increase as population in a specific, confined area increases?

The data

The US Department of Justice, through the Federal Bureau of Investigation, maintains crime statistics. In 2017 the FBI estimated that just under 1.25 million violent crimes were committed in the US, a country with a population estimated that year to be

---

[27] Assumptions are the Mother's Milk of research and unavoidable. I am working on a paper which will start by assuming it contains no mistakes.

318.5 million. This turns into a crime rate of just less than four tenths of 1% per person. Since it is hard to commit four tenths of one percent of a crime, crime statistics are often reported as number of crimes per 100,000 population. So, in 2017 the US had a crime rate of 392 per 100,000.

What can we learn?

If we claim that crime rises with increased population, the state with the lowest population should have the lowest crime rate. But Wyoming, the least populous of the 48 contiguous states, is tenth in crime rate so that does not work. Maine has the lowest crime rate and it is the tenth least populous state. AHA!! We have found the connection!! Not really. Vermont is the second least populous state and it has – you guessed it – the second lowest crime rate. We've done it. We have proved our point. Men are all animals!!

Sorry, **MISTAKE**. The conclusion may still be right but not because of these data. The state with the third lowest crime rate, New Hampshire, is the ninth least populous state. The state with the least density, Alaska, has the highest crime rate. [28] California is the most populous but is 15th from the top in crime.

It is time for some graphics. Suppose we pair up each state's population and crime rate and show

---

[28] Wyoming has the smallest population of any state. Alaska has the smallest number of people per unit of land mass.

those pairs on a plot with x (horizontal axis) as the population and y (vertical axis) as the crime rate. Adding what we know about a few states, it is evident (to me) that we don't know much about how crowding affects crime.

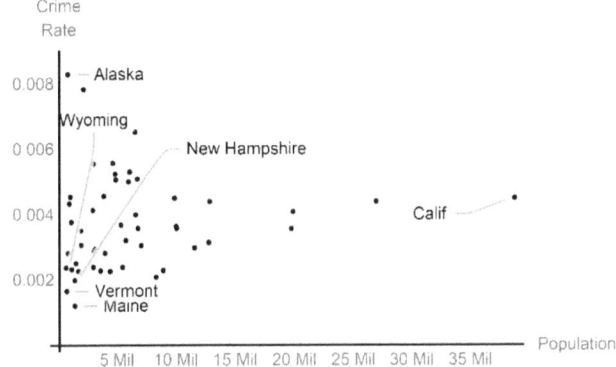

Digression: Linear Relationships

Life is a straight line. Really???? Anyone over the age of 12 knows (or should know) that statement is not true. It is a mistake to believe that life is linear. Certainly, no married person believes it. The false assumption underlying this very common error is that output is proportional to input. This condition, however convenient, is amazingly rare. Two cases are shown below. On the top, if you put in radius you get out diameter by multiplying by a constant number known as π.[29] Change the radius a little bit and the diameter changes by π times that little bit.

---

[29] This may be just a constant number, but it is no ordinary number. π is a *transcendental* number entire books have been written about.

Likewise, on the bottom, with temperature measured on the Celsius scale. Up it a little bit and Fahrenheit goes up by 9/5 times that little bit (after you add 32 to start). The result is a linear relationship between the value on the x axis and the value on the y axis. Note the <u>line</u> goes perfectly through a series of dots all <u>line</u>d up on the <u>line</u>. Those dots represent various points "sampled" from measuring different circles or different temperatures. One of the reasons this is so rare is that, in these cases, theory and practice are perfectly aligned. One supports the other without exception. Do not expect to find many of these relationships.

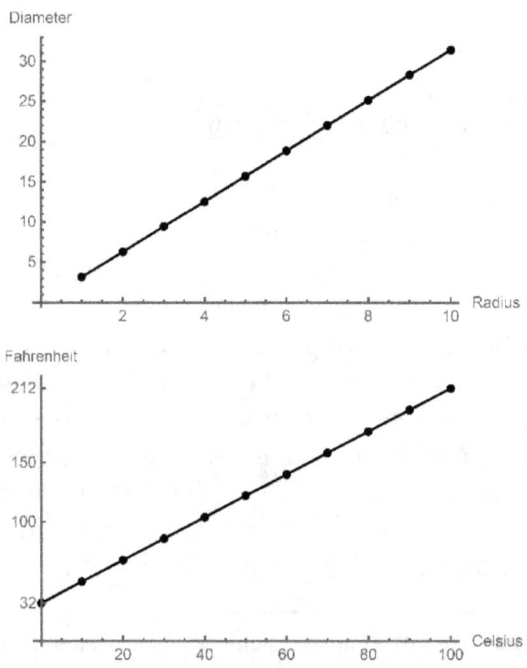

I deliberately chose two *physical* quantities for the plots above. In physics you can find some linear relationships. Things change when you introduce people. Linearity is generally out the window for the social sciences. That does not stop the social engineers from torturing the mathematics to get the result they want.[30]

Below are two non-linear plots. First, we see the path of the average undergraduate male as he goes through his day.

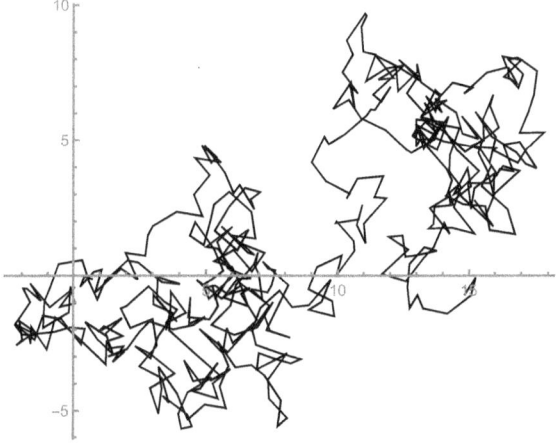

Next is a more well-behaved but non-linear plot that obeys a specific functional form known as a sine wave.

---

[30] Cf. Stuart Ritchie's wonderful and sobering book <u>Science Fictions, How Fraud, Bias, Negligence and Hype Undermine the Search for Truth</u>, Metropolitan Books, 2020.

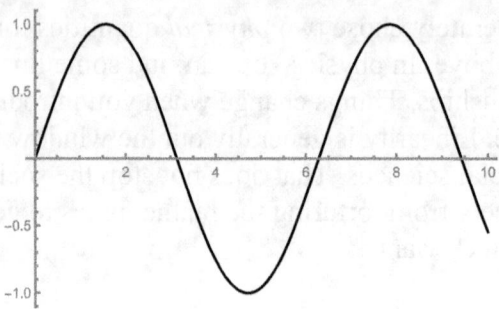

Both are more common than linear relationships.

Here is an excellent example of a simple mistake a lot of people make every day. The "gig" economy has produced thousands of rideshare (Uber, Lyft, etc.) drivers. Some of these think they are getting free money from their cellphone just for driving around. Some of the smarter ones realize they must go to the gas station more often when they hire out their car. Some even smarter realize they have to go to their mechanic more often. These people are smart to consider the cost of driving their car for money. They are doing what is known as a "cost-benefit" analysis, something widely respected in business and engineering. Some of the smartest know that one day they will have to throw their car into the trash can *and that day is closer to today if I rideshare my car*. Underlying this is the recognition that a car is a wasting asset that will someday reach the end of its useful life and no longer serve its purpose as transportation.

Some even smarter geeks figured out how to harness cellphone, credit card and GPS technology to create rideshare apps. Good for them. Perhaps the smartest thing they did was design a taxi company *without having to buy any cars*. Thus, the question of vehicle useful life is unimportant to Uber or Lyft. It is the drivers' problem. There are now several websites that offer so-called "true cost of rideshare behavior" of varying accuracy.

It is a mistake to miss the fact that the average is *linear*. Suppose that we all agree that no car lasts forever and that all cars fail at some time in the future after years of use and miles driven. What we do not agree on is *the rate at which its usefulness declines.* In the plot below you see two lines. The upper one is straight, the lower, thicker one is curved. The end of life occurs at the same time for both lines. What is overlooked is that predictions are about the average. Your mileage may vary. No, your mileage WILL vary. So will the life of your vehicle. Anyone who predicted an average outcome along a straight line and got something less along the curved line bears a cost of prediction error.[31] Thus, the genius of rideshare founders is to exploit this mistake on a massive scale.

---

[31] Sam Savage has written a wonderful book titled <u>The Flaw of Averages</u> using lots of examples of this error. Sam did not invent this, it was described by Johan Jensen in 1906. Named "Jensen's Inequality" it is considered one of the major contribution to mathematics and information science.

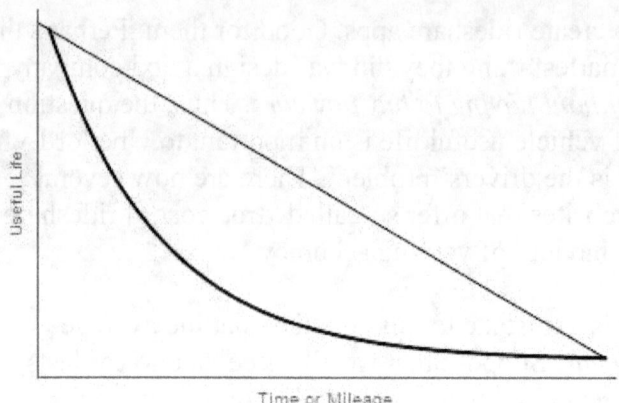

A very common mistake

Every time you hear or read "Studies show…" there is a large probability that what follows is a mistake. Many a graduate student with a dataset and a computer has "found" linear relationships that are very questionable and still had them published. The Boy Scout knife of statistical analysis is a tool known as linear regression. There are a few simple formulae that purport to "show" how two sets of numbers are related. Let's crank up our computer and make some mistakes with our FBI data.

Correlation

There is an old joke about the man who took his wife's birth control pills and, sure enough, six months later he was not pregnant. This joke is told (along with many others like it) to illustrate the concept that correlation is *not* causation. It is a mistake to think that just because two numbers are highly correlated one *causes* the other. The usual metric that describes correlation is Pearson's Correlation Coefficient, a number between -1 (perfect negative correlation) and 1 (perfect positive correlation). In the middle is zero, indicating no correlation. The closer to zero we get (approaching from either side) the less we believe the two numbers are correlated at all.

Regression

Below is the same plot of points we have been using, showing population and crime rates for each of 50 states. Added this time is a solid line which "relates" the two. The x axis, Population, is called the input variable; the y axis, Crime Rate, is called the response variable. We are asking how the response variable changes with changes in the input variable? Does crime increase with population increase, if so, how? The line through the points is supposed to answer these questions.

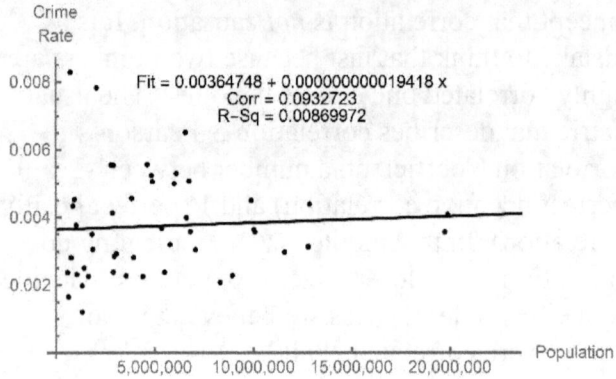

At this stage the most we can say is that there is a faint positive (the line slopes barely upward) relationship between population and crime. Yes, crime increases with population, but very little. That number with the ten zeros in front of it is the "little bit" analogous to our radius and temperature examples above. The implication (probably a mistake) is that every new birth (net of deaths) causes crime to increase by .00000000001941. Correlation, less than 10%, and R-Sq (the extent to which changes in population "explain" changes in crime rates), less than 1%, are both small, indicating that population is only marginally related to crime.

[This is where I ask for the reader's patience. Trust me, there is a bottom line here that ties the whole mistake-making business together in the end. I just need a bit more time to develop the foundation.]

<u>Yet another mistake</u>

It is a mistake to ask the wrong question or define

our terms casually. Perhaps the best message is that it is a mistake to be sloppy. Asking the right question precisely involves genuine talent.

Population is only one way to describe crowding. Most studies of crowding in the natural sciences are about cages or limited food supplies. Suppose we imagine that each state in the US has a wall completely surrounding it with no door for entering or exiting.[32] Crowding could then be described in terms of the population density (people divided by area). Since we know how many square miles are in each state and the population of each state, we can easily compute density. To make the scale of each axis similar we will measure people in the same "lumps" of 100,000. Below, the y axis is the same as before; the x axis is 100,000 people per square mile.

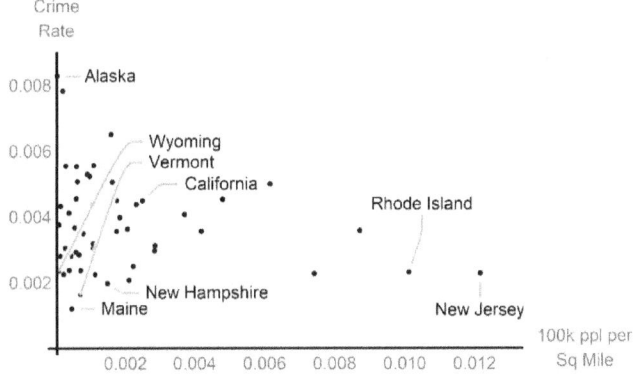

---

[32] Some would say it is a mistake to think we could do this. Others would do this around whole countries. Regardless, we also have to assume away airplanes and boats. Just go with me for the moment.

Note some big changes from the earlier plot. Particularly compare the two for the location of California. Conversely, many are in relatively the same position.

Repeating our earlier mistake, we again run the regression calculation on our new pairs of data. What do we "find"? Below, crime goes *down* as the number of people per unit of land increases!! This is counterintuitive. Worse, it "proves" the opposite of our pre-conceived notion. We can't have this, so we find another undergraduate to run the numbers again.

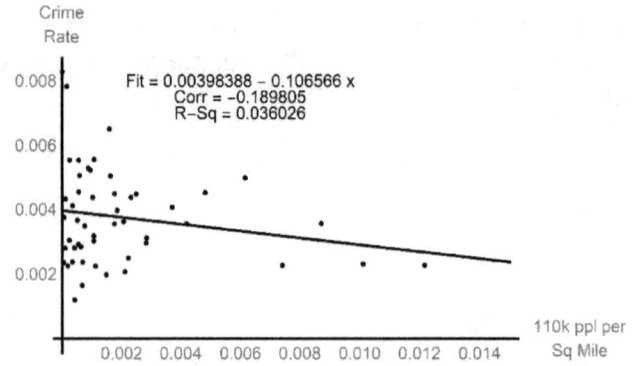

Inverting variables

In a fit of unmatched brilliance, we decide how many people there are per square mile is not what *really* matters. Rather, crime is influenced by how much "elbow room" citizens have. We want to compare crime rates to square feet available to each citizen. Below is our result.

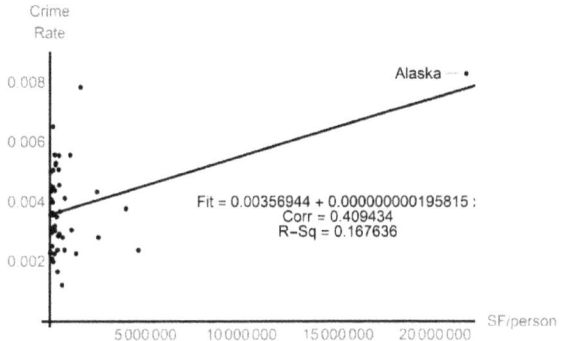

Finally, we have a decent correlation, just over 40%, and the line is pointing in the right direction. Or is it? Doesn't the plot say that crime *increases* with more elbow room? Yep, that is what it says. Essentially, area per person is just the inverse of people per area.

There is also a clue to why the line is steeper this time. Regression measures something called the conditional mean, which is just the average conditioned upon knowing some other information. It is well known that the average is strongly affected by extreme values far distant from the other values. Notice that the highest crime rate is in Alaska, a state offering the most (21,593,411 sf) land per person of all the states. One would think crime would be non-existent. Not so. Apparently, crime is affected by cold. The presence of that data point skews the general conclusion involving all the other states.

What have we learned? You can prove anything with numbers? Perhaps, but underlying assumptions and theory matter. Do "Studies show"? Sometimes not. The truth is that fake news is often just sloppy mistakes using data. This may disappoint some conspiracy theorists as a conspiracy to be stupid still requires some smarts.

There are many other criticisms to be made. Data only contain *reported* cases of violent crimes. Many go unreported. It is questionable to attribute an increase in crime to only a single factor, population. Economic factors such as unemployment play a role. Weather can be involved if one believes hot climates produce more crime when tempers flare (unless you are in Alaska). Then there is a time element which we have ignored in favor of the snapshot in time that 2017 represents.[33]

Enough with beating up on undergraduates and linear regression. It is time to turn ourselves to what we came for: Understanding how the internet trolls are getting to you.

Reverend Bayes find redemption

Long ago on a planet far away two kinds of people

---

[33] There is an excellent blog post here in which David Steinmetz, employing better data and more talent than I possess, describes how crime rates change in the same area over time.
https://www.datasciencecentral.com/profiles/blogs/the-pressure-cooker-population-density-and-crime

occupied Probableland, the place where predictions are made. There were the Frequentists and the Bayesians (the latter named after the cleric and mathematician Thomas Bayes). A great struggle over who was right persisted for hundreds of years. The Frequentists believed in collecting copious data, using their computers to process those data through their continuous models, and making predictions based on the *weight of the evidence*. Bayesians, on the other hand, believed that having whatever data was available at the moment constituted a useful starting point and the addition of another observation (data point) allowed one to update one's information set and adjust *degree of belief* to a more accurate position based on the new evidence. For most of time, with the help of academic politics (see Chapter 8) the Frequentists held sway. Lo, verily, they published more papers, got tenure sooner, were promoted and generally looked askance, over their glasses and down their beak-like noses at the lowly Bayesians.

Along came the internet. Then cellphones. Shortly after, Big Data arrived. Climate change came to Probableland and Reverend Bayes, though dead for a couple of centuries, found new life. For years the Frequentists had been bending curves as best they could, making them as straight as possible to support their linear continuous models. They forgot the fact that the lines of continuous models are just many points set really close together. Discrete models are just points with no connecting lines. Maybe in the physical and biological sciences you get lines, but elsewhere they are a fiction! Either way, POINTS matter. Bayesians, their minds neither dulled by tenure nor clouded by academic politics, saw the points for what they were: reality. Suddenly, with most of the civilized World carrying around large amounts of digital memory and processing power in the palm of their hand, every swipe or mouse click became a data point. Within nanoseconds an internet search for an Ocean Cruise vacation magically produced advertisements for luggage just to the right of the search results. A new age of advertising was born. With it came legions of geeks with machine learning, artificial intelligence and algorithms designed to nudge one's search in the direction the computer preferred over what the schmuck holding the mouse wanted.

On the surface it seemed like the last faltering step in the Decline and Fall of Western Civilization as we know it. What it really was is simpler and less ominous. It was and is a revolution brought about by *a collapse of the cost of prediction.*

Let's revisit our FBI data with Reverend Bayes by our side.

The new normal

One night not long ago I was having dinner with friends of the Jewish faith when one of them proclaimed that 52% of all hate crimes were perpetrated against Jewish people. This struck me as unlikely given the relatively small proportion Jews make of the overall US population. This also represented an excellent opportunity to apply Bayesian analysis.

In general, Bayes Rule is

$$P(A|B) = \frac{P(B|A)P(A)}{P(B)}$$
where A and B are events and $P(B) \neq 0$

- P(A) and P(B) are, respectively, the probability of observing A and the probability of observing B without regard to each other
- P(A|B) is the conditional probability of observing event A given that event B is true
- P(B|A) is the conditional probability of observing event B given that event A is true

Our question is the numerical value of P(A|B), the probability that a hate crime is observed (A) given that the victim is Jewish (B).

P(A) is the probability of a hate crime regardless of any characteristic of the victim. This would be the number of hate crimes divided by the eligible population. Problematic, perhaps, because it requires segregating hate crimes from all crimes and all crimes would include such things as misdemeanors and white-collar crime, incidents that probably do not rise (sink?) to the level of hate crime. Must a hate crime be violent? Is Holocaust Denial a crime? Is it a hate crime? There is more to be asked here as it has always bothered me to make some crimes worse because the victim is a member of any particular class. Is someone who is not in a special class less violated when the same fate befalls them? This is a hard question, but a different hard question than what we contemplate here. Someone else (the FBI) compiles data on this so they must know. I digress.

P(B) is the probability of drawing a Jewish person out of the pool of all people. Please do not take this literally as it is not about how Jewish people swim. Use "group" instead of "pool" if you prefer. This has all sorts of difficulties because hate crimes may be defined differently in different places, they may be perpetuated against property, etc. I suppose we can limit it to the US where the definition is constant and ***assume*** if the crime is against property and the owner of that property is Jewish, then it is a hate crime against a person of the Jewish faith.

There is also the sticky problem of randomness. Many crimes are crimes of passion where clearly the victim and perpetrator knew each other so the victim was chosen not because of his/her faith but because the perpetrator knew him/her. In the case of married people of the same faith who do violence to each other, isn't that [name of faith] on [same name of faith] crime? Wouldn't all crimes of passion be hate crimes? Does anyone manifest passion of the opposite sort by committing Love Crime? Now I'm just getting silly.

P(B|A) is the probability that one observes a Jewish

person, given that person has been the victim of a hate crime. Stated differently it is the probability that a victim of a hate crime is Jewish.

Restricting our study to the USA, the Jewish population is approximately 6.1 million (and that number is subject to lots of controversy, so one wonders if accuracy is EVER possible). There are about 319 million US citizens so about 0.019122 or $P(B) =$ just under 2% of the US population is Jewish.

FBI statistics on hate crimes introduce the single- and multi-bias terminology (you are Jewish and drive a Ford, is the crime against your religion or your choice of car?), further complicating the matter. For simplicity, let's just deal with single bias incidents.

Single-bias incidents (Based on Table 1.)

Analysis of the 5,818 single-bias incidents reported in 2015 revealed that:

- 56.9 percent were motivated by a race/ethnicity/ancestry bias.
- 21.4 percent were prompted by religious bias.
- 18.1 percent resulted from sexual-orientation bias.
- 2.0 percent were motivated by gender-identity bias.
- 1.3 percent were prompted by disability bias.
- 0.4 percent (23 incidents) were motivated by a gender bias.

Here is where a lesser man might attempt to re-write history to suggest that what I heard my friend say was somehow different from what my friend actually said. My research turned up this small factoid, an example of how casual statements made in haste can so easily be miss-repeats of summaries of otherwise valid data:

> *Religious bias (Based on Table 1.)*
> Hate crimes motivated by religious bias accounted for 1,354 offenses reported by law enforcement. A breakdown of the bias motivation of religious-biased offenses showed:
> - 51.3 percent were anti-Jewish.

Ignoring the math disconnect (5818 * .214 is 1,245 not 1,354 but that may have to do with the multi-bias incidents problem), let's just use the absolute numbers. $P(B|A) = 1354 * .513 = 694 \approx .12 * 5818 = 698$ so the conditional probability of someone being Jewish given that they have been involved in a hate crime is about 12%.

P(A), the probability of observing a hate crime seems like trouble, too. The probability of observing ANY crime is low. But if one has a pool of crimes (however defined) and draws one randomly there is some chance of drawing a hate crime that is higher than observing a hate crime among all observations, criminal or non-criminal.[34]

---

[34] This, the alert reader no doubt will quickly notice, is a variant of the Conjunction Fallacy central to the results of Tversky and Kahneman, one of whom was awarded the Nobel Prize in Economics in 2002 for this work. All are well advised to read <u>Thinking Fast and Slow</u> by Kahneman AND <u>The Undoing Project</u> by Michael Lewis, both of which are excellent not just because they eloquently describe why one might rightfully be confused at this moment.

Here is FBI information on the source of the data used above.

Population group	Agencies participating in UCR hate crime reporting	
	Number of participating agencies	Population covered
Total	14,997	283,884,034
Group I (Cities 250,000 and over)	76	57,352,602
Group II (Cities 100,000 - 249,999)	204	30,370,614
Group III (Cities 50,000 - 99,999)	452	31,527,813
Group IV (Cities 25,000 - 49,999)	811	27,948,918
Group V (Cities 10,000 - 24,999)	1,682	26,827,673
Group VI[1] (Cities under 10,000)	7,764	22,639,493
Metropolitan Counties[1]	1,690	64,161,388
Nonmetropolitan Counties[1]	2,318	23,055,533

[1] Includes universities and colleges, state police agencies, and/or other agencies to which no population is attributed.

This leaves us with P(A) = 5818/283,884,034 = .000020494 is the chance of being a victim of a hate crime. With all the ingredients we can finally compute the answer we seek.

$$P(A|B) = \frac{P(B|A)P(A)}{P(B)} = \frac{.12 * .000020494}{.019122} = .0001286$$

So my dinner companion misspoke and by a lot. Just over one hundredth of one percent of all hate crimes are against Jewish people. BUT 51.3 percent of hate crimes motivated by religious bias *are* directed at Jewish people. We can also use parts of the equation above to conclude that Jews are 6.27 times more likely to be a victim of a hate crime than a randomly selected person.

$$\frac{P(A|B)}{P(A)} = \frac{.0001286}{.000020494} = 6.27$$

This exercise illustrates many things. One is never have dinner with me. Another is how easy it is to manufacture fake news. What may be a small calculation error or slip of the tongue results in a very large difference in fact but that does not stop it from becoming a headline. Equally important, is how long it took to get this answer right. Finally, we are not home safe yet. Having the math right is good but it begs additional questions. My guess is that crimes of all sorts against affluent people are more likely to be reported, which is the only way these numbers appear in the data. If Jewish people are more likely to be affluent it is more likely that crimes of all sorts against them are reported. At a finer level the "tagging" of a crime as a hate crime may be related to the persistence of the victim to have it so reported. A culture that values persistence may influence more crimes against their tribe to be labeled hate crimes than, say for instance, Lutherans.

Why the Geeks are winning

Fasten your seat belt. We are going to take a leap at this point. We are going to jump over years of machine learning, decades of artificial intelligence and a century of *real* thinking about the subject at hand. These are casualties of simplification. Data scientists will want to close their eyes about now to avoid nausea.

Imagine that our data is not US national crime rates from the FBI. Rather it is Amazon's computer monitoring your keystrokes and mouse clicks and those of millions of your neighbors. Watch carefully. Notice that my fingers never leave my hand. You are planning a vacation on an ocean cruise. You are checking out destinations, prices, cruise liner amenities and the like. How long does it take? An hour? Maybe less? How many web pages or mouse clicks? Let's suppose you make 49 electronic "moves" that register at Google, each of which is tracked. The data look like what you see below. Not that you want to go to Alaska. No, it's that someone has paid to peer into your activities and, *using Bayesian probability mathematics*, has moved the needle just enough to encourage you to – while you are at it – investigate what new luggage would cost.

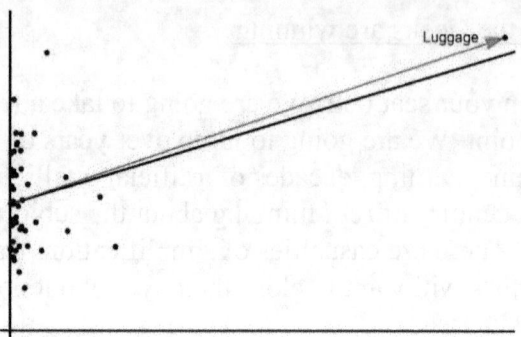

The technical term here is "Nudge" which does not sound very technical.[35] What it lacks in formality it makes up in descriptiveness. You have just been "nudged" by the geeks. Their watching your every electronic move is how commerce in the internet age moves forward.

In the meantime, give yourself a round of applause. You have just proved that men are animals with luggage.

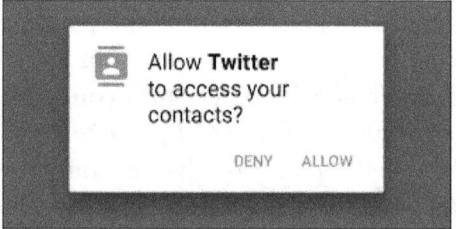

Allow. Be the first on your block.

---

[35] Perhaps, but it won Richard H. Thaler the Nobel Prize in Economics in 2017. He and Cass Sunstein wrote a book on just this one word. I am not reading his until he reads mine.

AFTERWORD

So, what shall we make from all of this? One thing is that an Afterword is a lot like the Foreword. It, too, is written last. Perhaps it serves to fill in blanks that may still not be in the body of the book.

This book is not about Dr. Pangloss lamenting a world full of heartless, brainless, spineless, violent people, crowded too close together, dominated by an evil, careless government. It is about being careful. Those who survive, even thrive, and contribute to those around them give serious thought to their motives and plans before they act. This is neither easy nor instantaneous. Failing *to take the time* to ponder carefully your life and actions can lead to (you guessed it!) mistakes.

In our household we have something we refer to with reverence as "The One Right Method." This is the way your Uncle Roger believes it (whatever "it" is) should be done. Thus, my well-deserved reputation as an impossible nitpicker. What is missed, in my own defense, is that I only recommend The One Right Method for one life, my own. Other people do things differently and provide me with a lot of entertainment. Well done, them! Still others want to apply their right method to you. These people are known as "Dangerous."

Maybe I have warned the reader about a number of things. Not an exhaustive list, clueless Bozos are still running about as you read this now, finding new ways of making mistakes. As their numbers increase you have to wonder what can be done to stop them.[36] It is worrisome that computers and government are evolving together using artificial intelligence in ways promising mistake-free solutions that offer the Grand Daddy of all Unintended Consequences. If you think about it, artificial intelligence is a mistake. It must be in order to be artificial.

Human beings are very resilient. Those of us with memories can remember when we all panicked decades ago at the thought of subliminal advertising. Back then we were worried that television would take over our lives. Today we think nothing of waking up in the morning to have Facebook tell us to brush our teeth with organic kale powder, Google tell us to call our mother and Alexa tell us to go to work.

Whatever you think is going to get you, it is something else. Not to worry, the mistake you are making now is just prologue. As long as you are letting someone else do your thinking for you, all will be well, or so it seems. We survived the fear of being dominated by television to become dominated by the internet. There will always be someone out there who wants to tell you want to do. The only thing that changes is the delivery system.

---

[36] The answer is: "Nothing." The Bible says somewhere "The poor ye shall always have with you." Nothing is said about the dumb. So much for the claim you can find anything in the Bible.

How to Make Mistakes

In Chapter 6 the question: "Who Shall Decide?" is mentioned. The sinister follow-up question is "Who Shall Decide For YOU?" If you have not already gotten the hint, your author believes that society achieves its best ends when individuals are as free as possible to seek their own best interest.[37] To close the circle on your author's predisposition in favor of using quantitative tools, think of individuals productively employing a grand number of ones and zeros for their own benefit as salvation. The key to fair and balanced news is to listen to NPR *and* FOX. Then do your own thinking.

I had a favorite professor in grad school who had a practice of summarizing each course with a list of what he called "Big Ideas" he wanted his students to take with them as they filed out the door at the end of the semester. Borrowing from him, here are three things that are central to the message of this book.

1. Systems are for averages, nothing more. If you want to stand out, you need to separate yourself from the crowd. Society has gravitated into a malaise that could be described as worshipping process over performance. We are bogged down with ill-conceived and poorly designed processes

---

[37] Adam Smith and others preceded me on this. See for instance a Google search of "The Invisible Hand" for lots of good information which may be viewed collectively as "How to Make the Minimum Number of Mistakes."

that interfere with getting anything done. People go to work, fill out forms and leave at 5 pm thinking their job is done, having done no job at all. They forget that there was once a time before all those forms, when we just followed simple rules of common decency, hard work and serving our customer. Somehow, life moved forward during those times. Today, good decisions arise from careful analysis of data. Whether we are better off under these conditions remains an open question;

and

2. Learn to measure things. I tried (and at least in Chapter 13 failed) to not make a big deal about math. But math is about measuring. The best decisions are best made when the subject matter can be measured. You can measure your height, weight and cholesterol. You can't measure how happy you are. You can, however, make comparisons between how happy you were yesterday and how happy you are today. You can also compare the relative happiness of you and your neighbor. If this leads you to lobby government to take something your neighbor owns and give it to you, this GIANT MISTAKE will lead inexorably to both of you being less happy. Your neighbor will have less to measure, and you will have

become dependent upon stolen property. The measure of your character will fall;

and

3. Never get involved with a Homeowner's Association.

ABOUT THE AUTHOR

Roger J. Brown, PhD has been an educator and consultant over more than 50 years in San Diego CA. He is the founder of www.mathestate.com. All of his formal schooling was received in the public education system. He is also the author of <u>The Worst of the Best of Roger J. Brown, Oeuvre of an Odd Thinker</u> and <u>Private Real Estate Investment, Data Analysis and Decision Making</u>.

ACKNOWLEDGEMENTS

The author wishes to thank his illustrator, Aaron Philby, without whose help this book would not be illustrated, and Kevin Dowd, who no doubt is embarrassed to be revealed as having read the whole thing and made valuable suggestions. Front cover inspired by an anonymous pavement striper. Back cover art by Dick Ranchero, professional garphic designer. Despite the help of all these brave souls, all mistakes remain proudly those of the author.

A special thanks goes to Herman Bierens, my last (?) math teacher, a man of heroic inspirational qualities matched only by his boundless patience. With me as a student he really needed the latter.

www.ingramcontent.com/pod-product-compliance
Lightning Source LLC
Chambersburg PA
CBHW072052290426
44110CB00014B/1655